The New Observer's Series
AUTOMOBILES

About the Book

Helpful to all who are interested in cars, this pocket book enables the user to recognise and identify most of the cars he sees, as well as providing all the 'vital statistics' about them. Notes on identity aim to guide the reader in distinguishing the model covered from other similar ones, and give brief introduction to the car, often mentioning the International Motor Show at which it first appeared for public scrutiny. All the key dimensions are given, covering such things as the engine's compression ratio and the size of the fuel tank. Under the 'Features' section, a summary of the model is given, or other special information such as main appeal of the model, or its equipment details.

Completely revised for 1985, *Observer's Automobiles* is right up to date, even including some models such as the Mercedes-Benz 300E which was not announced in Germany until December 1984. In the total of 180 cars featured in the 1985 edition—each illustrated by an up-to-date picture—are a representative coverage of the products of all the leading manufacturers of the world (as well as some small ones such as Bitter, Bristol and TVR), plus a number of fascinating and rarely seen 'exotics'. Thus you can read about the new Ferrari Testarossa, the Marcos Mantula, Lancia Delta HF Turbo, or the Dacia Duster.

This pocket-size book is an invaluable instant reference to answer most of your queries on car recognition and improve your motoring knowledge.

About the Author

Stuart Bladon has been an enthusiast for cars of all kinds ever since he had to be forcibly removed from his first 'car', made of sand at the seaside, when he was only 4. Aged 8, he started driving by working the clutch, gear lever and steering from the passenger seat for an understanding aunt who was on essential work and able to get petrol during the war. As a National Service officer he was in charge of a platoon of staff cars and ambulances, and in 1955 went straight from there to the editorial staff of the weekly motoring magazine *The Autocar*.

In 26 years with the magazine he drove and Road Tested all manner of cars, and was Deputy Editor when he left in 1981 to become a freelance motoring and travel writer. His enthusiasm for cars and motoring remains undiminished and he covers all developments in new models and writes Road Tests and other motoring articles for a number of outlets at home and abroad. He has the advantage that he has personal experience of driving most of the cars analysed in this book.

W9-CJM-770

The New Observer's Book of
Automobiles

Compiled by
Stuart Bladon

Frederick Warne

FREDERICK WARNE

Penguin Books Ltd, Harmondsworth, Middlesex, England
Viking Penguin Inc., 40 West 23 Street, New York,
New York, 10010, U.S.A.
Penguin Books Australia Ltd, Ringwood, Victoria, Australia
Penguin Books Canada Ltd, 2801 John Street, Markham,
Ontario, Canada L3R 1B4
Penguin Books (N.Z.) Ltd, 182-190 Wairau Road, Auckland
10, New Zealand

First edition 1955
Twenty-eighth edition 1985

Copyright © Frederick Warne & Co Ltd, London 1985

NOTE

The specifications contained in this book were collated on
the basis of material available to the compiler up to the end
of December 1984. All information is subject to change
and/or cancellation during the course of the model year.
Although every effort has been made to ensure accuracy in
compiling this book responsibility for errors and omissions
cannot be accepted by the compilers and publishers.

ISBN 0-7232-1675-4

Printed and bound in Great Britain by
William Clowes Limited, Beccles and London

CONTENTS

Land Rover	90 94; Range Rover Vogue 95
Lincoln	Continental 96
Lotus	Eclat Excel 97; Esprit 98; Etna 99
Marcos	Mantula 100
Mazda	MX-02 101; 626 102; RX-7 103
Mercedes-Benz	190D 104; 190E 16V 105; 300E 106; 380 SEC 107; 500SL 108
Mercury	Cougar 109; Marquis 110
MG	Maestro EFi 111; Metro Turbo 112; Montego EFi 113
Mitsubishi	Cordia Turbo 114; Colt 1600 115; Lancer 1500 GLX 116; Space Wagon 117; Starion 118
Morgan	Plus 8 119
Naylor	MG TF 1700 Replica 120
Nissan	Bluebird 121; Silvia Turbo ZX 122; 300ZX Turbo 123; Prairie 124
Oldsmobile	Calais 125; Cutlass Ciera 126; Firenza GT Coupé 127; Toronado Caliente 128
Opel	Manta GTE 129; Monza GSE 130
Panther	Kallista 2.8i 131
Peugeot	205 GTI 132; 305 GTX 133; 505 GLD Diesel Estate car 134
Pininfarina	Spidereuropa GT 135
Plymouth	Gran Fury 136
Pontiac	Fiero 137; Sunbird LE convertible 138; Firebird 139
Porsche	911 Carrera Cabriolet 140; 944 141; 928S Series 2 142
Reliant	Scimitar SS-1 143; Scimitar GTC convertible 144
Renault	5GTL 145; 11 Turbo 146; Fuego GTX Turbo 147; 25 GTX 148
Rolls-Royce	Corniche convertible 149; Silver Spirit 150
Rover	213 Vanden Plas 151; Vitesse 152
Saab	900 Turbo Cabriolet 153; 9000 Turbo 16V 154
Seat	Ibiza 155
Skoda	Rapid Cabriolet 156
Subaru	1800 4WD 157; L-Series 1.8 GTi 158
Suzuki	Alto 159; SJ4 10WV 4 × 4 160
Talbot	Horizon Pullman 161; Matra Murena 162; Rancho 163; Rapier 164; Samba Cabriolet 165
Toyota	Camry 1.8 Turbo diesel 166; Carina 1.6 GL 167; 1600GT Coupé 168; Celica 2.0 XT Coupé 169; Corolla GL Liftback 170; MR2 171; Model F 172; Supra 173; Tercel 4WD 174
TVR	390SE convertible 175
Vauxhall	Astra SR 176; Carlton CD 177; Cavalier 1.8 CD 178; Cavalier 1.6 Estate Car 179; Nova 1.2 GL Hatchback 180; Senator 3.0i CD 181
Volkswagen	Golf 1.6 GL 182; Golf GTI 183; Jetta 1.3 Formel E 184; Passat 4 × 4 185; Passat GL5 186; Polo 187; Scirocco Storm 188
Volvo	360 GLE injection 189; 240 Estate Car 190; 740 191
Yugo	45 GL 192

COUNTRY OF MANUFACTURE

The letter (or letters) following the make of car indicates the country of manufacture. These are:

AUS	Australia	J	Japan
CH	Switzerland	K	Korea
CS	Czechoslovakia	P	Poland
D	German Federal Republic	S	Sweden
E	Spain	SU	USSR
F	France	USA	United States of America
GB	United Kingdom	YU	Yugoslavia
I	Italy		

AMERICAN AND METRIC

In last year's edition, I advanced the theory that the reason why the US gallon is smaller than the British one is because some of the contents of the 'standard gallon' which the early explorers took across with them had either spilt or evaporated by the time they had completed the hazardous crossing of the Atlantic. This, I am assured, is not correct; and what actually happened was that one of the crew thought it was the drinking water, and had substantially lowered the contents by the time he was caught drinking from it, and reprimanded.

Be this as it may, the important point is that the US gallon.is only 0.83 of the Imperial one. All mpg figures throughout the book are to the Imperial gallon, and should be divided by 1.2 to obtain distance that would be travelled on a US gallon. Fuel tank contents need to be multiplied by 1.2 to obtain the US value.

Even though most garages in Britain now sell fuel by the litre, motorists still assess consumption as miles per gallon; and miles per litre (simply multiply the mpg figure by 0.22) still means little to anyone. Even less widely used is the Continental measurement of consumption as litres per 100 kilometres (l/100 km); but if this is needed, divide the mpg figure into 282.5.

Other differences from the American terminology have been enumerated before, and do not usually cause confusion. In particular, the American car's suspension *shocks* are known as *dampers*; and the *ISO strut* is termed *MacPherson strut*. Carburettor *barrel* is *choke*.

ABOUT THE 1985 EDITION

Here we are with the third in the new series of *Observer's Automobiles*, and again the aim has been to continue steady improvement and tidying-up of the content, following the major overhaul of 1983. In a bid to make the order more logical, all measurements and statistics are given in Imperial first, followed by the metric conversion where appropriate. Some metric conversions not previously given, such as the speed at 1000 rpm in top gear, are included for the first time.

So many cars now have power assistance for their steering, that this has been made a routine entry following the type of steering, so that the reader can see at a glance if power steering is standard.

It is hoped that collectors of the series will approve these small changes, without any dramatic alteration in content or format. A few of the entries are carried over from last year, where they were considered to be still significant; but the majority are new.

As in the past, a deliberate effort has been made to ensure topicality, by including such cars as the Audi 200 Quattro Avant and the Mercedes-Benz 300E, which were announced late in the year and are newly in production at the beginning of 1985. Also, by way of a little light amusement, some strange cars not in production have been included, such as the Citroen ECO 2000 and the Mazda MX-02.

Once again I must record how appalled I am at the shocking inadequacy of the information provided by US manufacturers about their cars. It seems that one must be content to learn that there is a new grab rail for the passenger, or a relocated decal on the side, and accept that basic technical details about the type of engine or suspension are considered too unimportant to mention.

This disinterest on matters which are regarded as of considerable importance by the European buyer perhaps goes some way towards explaining the mediocre road behaviour of many American cars against their European counterparts.

Similarly, data on maximum speed and acceleration of American cars is generally shaky or not available at all, and even fuel consumption data is vague and uninformative.

Whatever one may think of the European 'official fuel figures', including the haphazard 'urban' figures, they have at least achieved a measure of uniformity over fuel consumption claims.

An unexpected event of the year was the sale by my former empoyers of the motoring magazine *Autocar*, with resultant change of Editor. I am delighted that the change has not prevented me from continuing to quote the copyright Road Test figures of acceleration, top speed and overall fuel consumption; permission to use this data where available has kindly been given by the new Editor.

Where Road Test data is not available because the car has not yet been tested by the journal, the term 'Works' indicates that manufacturer's figures are quoted; and if the manufacturer is in America, then usually a brave attempt has had to be made to estimate it.

ANOTHER FRUITFUL NEW MODEL YEAR

'You seem to be always away trying new cars,' I was told; well, it certainly began to seem like it during 1984—a year which brought more new model announcements in Europe than even the record year of 1983 had produced. Car manufacturers are well aware that they have to keep striving for perfection to keep in business, and this leads to the inevitable replacement of a model range after an ever-shorter cycle. Many manufacturers are even well down the road on the design for a successor before a new model has even been launched to the public.

In other words, the new model you may read about on a particular day will already be obsolete as far as its designers are concerned! This is because technology will have changed even in the relatively short time since work on it first started—perhaps four or five years earlier. The good result of all this activity is that cars go on getting better and better as their creators discover new ways to improve the product, and that there is scarcely a dull moment for an observer of the motoring scene and its industry.

Last year I recorded that there had been 40 new models; this year, the total is over 50. Again it has been my job to co-ordinate a team of three judging panels and compile a list of the Top Ten of the year's new models, from which the Guild of Motoring Writers pick the year's Top Car for the Award sponsored by United Dominions Trust.

It was a fascinating task. The first six places were quickly filled by the obvious prime contenders: but then there were about 12 models, all very deserving, which had to be whittled down for the remaining four places.

Some of the finalists, such as the Renault 25, had already featured in the 1984 edition of this book, as I had been able to get details of them in advance; others were new in the year. Eligibility for the Guild's award runs from the beginning of November to the end of October, so the new Mercedes-Benz W124 range, which I have managed to include in this edition, will not be judged for the Guild's Top Car until the 1986 Award.

In addition to the Renault 25 which I have mentioned already, the other nine which 'made the final' were: Austin and MG Montego, Honda Civic, Hyundai Stellar, Mitsubishi Hatchback Turbo, Peugeot 205GTI, Rover 213, Toyota Carina, Vauxhall Astra (and the Opel Kadett, as it is known on the Continent), and the Volkswagen Golf.

Following selection, the members of the Guild—which includes nearly all who are involved in motoring writing, photography or broadcasting in Britain, as well as in many countries overseas— were able to vote on the short-listed cars, and on any other models if they wished.

By a clear lead, the Award went to the Renault 25. Runners-up were the Austin/MG Montego, Peugeot 205GTI and Volkswagen Golf. No classification is revealed for runners-up. The result delighted me, as I am a great admirer of the new big Renault as a very comfortable and roomy car, with high efficiency: it performs well, yet does not require a great deal of fuel—and that is the target at which all manufacturers are aiming.

When I heard that the Peugeot 205GTI had also finished as one of the runners-up, I recalled flying in to Spain during the year to drive this new model. The test route went over a very demanding mountain course, on which I had a most enjoyable drive, revelling in the delightfully crisp and responsive handling, light yet dead accurate steering, and superb performance of this new three-door version of the Peugeot 205 hatchback, boosted by fuel injection for its engine.

Inclusion of the Volkswagen Golf as runner-up was also well-deserved. I was so impressed by this new four-door hatchback when I tried it in January that I decided to buy one—and it certainly has not disappointed. It uses less fuel, goes faster, seems roomier inside and yet is more compact externally, than the model I owned before. This sort of progress, surely, is what every manufacturer strives to achieve.

The other runner-up—Austin-MG's Montego—is a comfortable, roomy and pleasing car, which also deserved to do well.

A number of other new cars launched during the year made a big impression: not many were nondescript, and easily forgotten. Highlights were the Lancia Thema, the Mitsubishi hatchback turbo, the new Mercedes-Benz W124 models, and a whole range of new Audis with four-wheel drive, all sporting the name Quattro.

Roads were either streaming wet or covered in sheet ice when I tried these Audis. In such conditions, permanent four-wheel drive gives real benefit, making the car handle more securely, with better feeling of balance in its cornering behaviour, especially when climbing a steep gradient at the same time.

I feel sure that four-wheel drive is a development that will be seen much more often on the models of the future; makes which do not offer it yet, are no doubt working hard on development, to be able to provide it in the future. However, I do have to reprimand Audi for claiming that the Audi quattro represented the first application of permanent four-wheel drive in a production car. Long before Audi reached its present eminence, I remember driving out to Switzerland to test a British car with American Chrysler V8 engine and featuring drive to all four wheels using a system pioneered by the late Harry Ferguson. Its name: the Jensen FF.

All of the new Mercedes-Benz W124 range, which again I tried in Spain, impressed me with their meticulous attention to detail and their thorough engineering. Most outstanding of all was perhaps the 300D—the version with new big six-cylinder 3-litre diesel engine. By totally encapsulating the engine, Daimler-Benz have managed to suppress most of the unpleasant clatter which is so objectionable with most diesels. But it is the 300E, with the new six-cylinder 3-litre petrol engine, which I have included in the text, being the model in which I had a memorably fast and exciting drive in Spain.

Sadly, I remember more about driving the new BMW 518i, with

four-cylinder 1.8-litre engine which is expected to find special favour in Britain because it gets a low rating for company car tax, than I do about the exciting new M353i model. It is simply because the conditions were so bad—heavy rain, dark, and dense weekend traffic on the *autobahn* in Germany—that there was not much opportunity to exploit a 143 mph car. However, there is no doubt that the new BMW M535i is a magnificent machine—effortlessly fast—and it coped very well with the bad conditions during my Friday night drive from Munich to Austria.

Another very impressive new car of the year was the Lancia Thema range; and I have picked out the one which seemed particularly outstanding—the i.e. turbo. Lancia have had a rough time for some years and needed a really good car to help put them back into prosperity. The marque deserves to get a big boost from the Thema.

What of the lower end of the market? Main change has been introduction of the deserving and very soundly engineered little replacement for the Vauxhall Astra and Opel Kadett, bringing aerodynamic body styling to the small car. Other significant developments of the year included Fiat's clever little four-wheel drive version of the Panda, Renault's new 5 range, the little turbocharged Lancia Delta, and the four-door hatchback body for the Austin Metro.

Now on to the main review pages, covering a significant cross-section of the world's cars.

VAUXHALL (GB, D) | COVER CAR | Astra GTE

Identity: Top of the new Astra range is the exciting GTE version. Available only in three-door form, the model is powered by the 1800 injection engine. Easily distinguishable with front airdam and rear spoiler. Top competitor in the 'hot hatchback' class. Low-drag shape.

Engine: Front-mounted transverse four-cylinder with belt-driven single ohc. Hydraulic tappets. Bosch LE-Jetronic fuel injection. Bore 84.8 mm, stroke 79.5 mm; capacity 1796 cc. Power 115 bhp (85.7 kW) at 5800 rpm; torque 111.4 lb ft (154 Nm) at 4800 rpm. Compression 9.5-to-1.

Transmission: Front-wheel drive; five-speed manual gearbox; no automatic option. Top gear speed at 1000 rpm: 19.76 mph (31.8 km/h).

Suspension: Front, independent, MacPherson struts and coil springs; telescopic dampers. Heavy duty rubber mountings. Anti-roll bar. Rear, compound crank dead axle and miniblock coil springs; gas-filled telescopic dampers.

Steering: Rack and pinion. Power assistance: not available.

Brakes: Ventilated discs front, drums rear, servo-assisted.

Tyres: 185/60 HR-14.   **Fuel tank:** 9.2 Imp. gall (42 litres).

Dimensions: Length 157.4 in (3997 mm), width 66.5 in (1689 mm), height 54.9 in (1394 mm), wheelbase 99.2 in (2520 mm).

Unladen weight: 2094 lb (950 kg).

Performance (Works): Maximum speed 126 mph (203 km/h); 0 to 60 mph (100 km/h) 9.0 sec. Fuel consumption at constant 75 mph (120 km/h): 39.2 mpg.

Features: Highly distinctive sports appearance. A model that not only looks good but is also very satisfying to drive with a responsive engine and excellent handling characteristics. Sports seats and digital instruments.

ALFA ROMEO (I)   Alfa 33 Gold Cloverleaf

Identity: Launched in Britain mid-1983, as addition to Alfasud range but with larger body of four doors plus hatchback, the 33 does not continue the famous Alfasud name. Available with two engine sizes, 1.3- or 1.5-litre, two special editions, Gold Cloverleaf and Green Cloverleaf.

Engine: Front-mounted horizontally-opposed four-cylinder with single belt-driven overhead camshaft per bank. Twin-choke downdraught carb. Bore 84 mm, stroke 67.2 mm; capacity 1490 cc. Power 95 bhp (62.5 kW) at 5800 rpm; torque 96 lb ft (130 Nm) at 4000 rpm. Compression 9.0-to-1.

Transmission: Front-wheel drive; five-speed manual gearbox; no automatic option. Top gear speed at 1,000 rpm: 18.8 mph (30.3 km/h).

Suspension: Front, independent, MacPherson struts; coil springs and telescopic dampers. Anti-roll bar. Rear, dead beam axle on two longitudinal Watts linkages, with Panhard rod. Coil springs and telescopic dampers.

Steering: Rack and pinion. Power assistance: not available.

Brakes: Discs front and rear, servo-assisted.

Tyres: 165/70-13.   **Fuel tank:** 11.0 Imp. gall (50 litres).

Dimensions: Length 158.3 in (4022 mm), width 63.46 in (1612 mm), height 52.76 in (1340 mm), wheelbase 96.65 in (2455 mm).

Unladen weight: 1973 lb (895 kg).

Performance *Autocar* test: Maximum speed 111 mph (179 km/h); 0 to 60 mph (100 km/h) 9.8 sec. Fuel consumption at constant 75 mph (120 km/h): 37.7 mpg; overall test, 25.0 mpg.

Features: The famous Alfasud engine gives the Alfa 33 excellent performance and sporty response, and car offers very safe handling. Four-wheel drive version also available.

ALFA ROMEO (I)   90 Gold Cloverleaf

Identity: The Alfa 90 is intended to replace the ageing Alfetta. Based on the same chassis platform as the Alfetta, it has a new body, styled by Bertone, which combines design features of both the Alfetta and the Alfa 33. The Alfa 90 is to be the backbone of this Italian maker's model range, and the top version is the 90 Gold Cloverleaf.

Engine: Front-mounted V6-cylinder with Bosch L-Jetronic fuel injection. Bore 88 mm, stroke 68.3 mm; capacity 2492 cc. Power 156 bhp (116 kW) at 5600 rpm; torque 155 lb ft (210 Nm) at 4000 rpm. Compression 9.0-to-1.

Transmission: Rear-wheel drive; five-speed manual gearbox; no automatic option. Top gear speed at 1000 rpm: 25.4 mph (40.9 km/h).

Suspension: Front, independent, double wishbones. Longitudinal torsion bars. Telescopic dampers. Anti-roll bars front and rear. Rear, De Dion tube with Watts linkage. Telescopic dampers.

Steering: Rack and pinion. Power assistance: standard.

Brakes: Discs front and rear, servo-assisted.

Tyres: 195/60-15.   **Fuel tank:** 10.7 Imp. gall (49 litres).

Dimensions: Length 172.8 in (4391 mm), width 64.5 in (1638 mm), height 56 in (1420 mm), wheelbase 93.8 in (2510 mm).

Unladen weight: 2579 lb (1170 kg).

Performance (Works): Maximum speed 126 mph (203 km/h); 0 to 60 mph (100 km/h) 8.4 sec. Fuel consumption at constant 75 mph (120 km/h): 31.7 mpg.

Features: Interesting aerodynamic feature on the Alfa 90 is an adjustable front spoiler whose height is varied according to the car's speed. Model available with 1.8-, 2.0- (carb and fuel injected) and 2.4-litre turbo diesel versions, as well as the V6 2.5-litre Gold Cloverleaf.

AMERICAN MOTORS (USA)   Alliance

Identity: American-built version of the Renault 9. The two- or four-door saloon has minor styling differences from its French sister model. Mechanical details very similar, but the American version features Bendix or Bosch fuel injection and options for four or five-speed gearbox as well as three-speed automatic.

Engine: Front-mounted transverse four-cylinder with alloy head and cast iron block. OHV. Breakerless ignition. Bore 76 mm, stroke 77 mm; capacity 1397 cc. Power 60 bhp (45 kW) at 5000 rpm; torque 74 lb ft (100 Nm) at 3000 rpm. Compression 8.8-to-1.

Transmission: Front-wheel drive; four-speed manual gearbox; five-speed and automatic options. Top gear speed at 1,000 rpm: 22.1 mph (35.7 km/h).

Suspension: Front, independent, MacPherson struts, coil springs and telescopic dampers. Anti-roll bar. Rear, independent, trailing arms and transverse torsion bars. Telescopic dampers. Anti-roll bar.

Steering: Rack and pinion. Power assistance: optional extra.

Brakes: Discs front, drums rear, servo-assisted.

Tyres: 155/80-13.   **Fuel tank:** 12.5 Imp. gall (57 litres).

Dimensions: Length 163.8 in (4161 mm), width 65 in (1651 mm), height 54.4 in (1385 mm), wheelbase 97.8 in (2483 mm).

Unladen weight: 1969 lb (893 kg).

Performance *Autocar* test of UK version, GTL: Maximum speed 94 mph (151 km/h); 0 to 60 mph (100 km/h) 14.2 sec. Fuel consumption at constant 75 mph (120 km/h): 38.7 mpg; overall test, 32.4 mpg.

Features: High specification available, including electrically operated window lifts and air conditioning. Convertible bodywork (illustrated) also available.

AMERICAN MOTORS (USA)   Encore

Identity: American version of the Renault 11, launched 1983. As with the Alliance, there are slight styling changes but mechanically the Encore is very similar to its Continental cousin. Available in two- or four-door hatchback versions.

Engine: Front-mounted transverse four-cylinder with alloy head and cast iron block. OHV. Bendix or Bosch fuel injection. Bore 76 mm, stroke 77 mm; capacity 1397 cc. Power 60 bhp (45 kW) at 5000 rpm; torque 74 lb ft (100 Nm) at 3000 rpm. Compression 8.8-to-1.

Transmission: Front-wheel drive; four-speed manual gearbox; five speed and automatic options. Top gear speed at 1000 rpm: 22.1 mph (35.7 km/h).

Suspension: Front, independent, MacPherson struts, coil springs and telescopic dampers. Anti-roll bar. Rear, independent, trailing arms and transverse torsion bars. Telescopic dampers. Anti-roll bar.

Steering: Rack and pinion. Power assistance: optional extra.

Brakes: Discs front, drums rear, servo-assisted.

Tyres: 155/80-13.   **Fuel tank:** 12.5 Imp. gall (57 litres).

Dimensions: Length 160.6 in (4079 mm), width 65 in (1651 mm), height 54.4 in (1385 mm), wheelbase 97.8 in (2483 mm).

Unladen weight: 2010 lb (912 kg).

Performance *Autocar* test: of UK version (11 TSE): Maximum speed 95 mph (152 km/h); 0 to 60 mph (100 km/h) 12.8 sec. Fuel consumption at constant 75 mph (120 km/h): 36.2 mpg; overall test, 34.1 mpg.

Features: Versatility of split and folding rear seat, plus hatchback. Option of clever electronic lock and unlock key fob. Renault Monotrace front seat adjustment.

ASTON MARTIN (GB)   Lagonda V8 Tickford

Identity: Impressive luxury saloon with Aston Martin V8 engine. Extensive use of aluminium for body panels; separate steel chassis. An immensely satisfying car to drive; very fast, very safe, and magnificent on long journeys. This special Tickford version was launched in 1983.

Engine: Front-mounted V8-cylinder with twin ohc each bank. Alloy for block and heads; wet cylinder liners. Four Weber carbs. Bore 100 mm, stroke 85 mm; capacity 5340 cc. Power and torque: no figures quoted by Aston Martin.

Transmission: Rear-wheel drive; Chrysler Torqueflite automatic transmission standard (no manual version available). Top gear speed at 1000 rpm: 25.8 mph (41.5 km/h).

Suspension: Front, independent, coil springs and wishbones; telescopic dampers. Anti-roll bar. Rear, De Dion layout, with coil springs and telescopic dampers.

Steering: Rack and pinion. Power assistance: standard.

Brakes: Ventilated discs front and rear, servo-assisted.

Tyres: 235/70 VR 15.   **Fuel tank:** 28 Imp. gall (128 litres).

Dimensions: Length 208 in (5820 mm), width 70.5 in (1790 mm), height 51 in (1300 mm), wheelbase 115 in (2910 mm).

Unladen weight: 4459 lb (2023 kg).

Performance: Maximum speed 143 mph (230 km/h); 0 to 60 mph (100 km/h); 8.8 sec. Fuel consumption, 17.6 mpg at constant 75 mph (120 km/h).

Features: Lavish equipment including electric window lifts and air-conditioning. Digital intruments. Pop-up headlamps. US-style bumpers and under spoilers introduced for 1984, with better seats and improved control layout. Dual scale speedometer introduced 1985.

ASTON MARTIN (GB)   Volante

Identity: Still one of the few high performance convertibles which are also true four-seaters. Fabulously expensive but very desirable, and improved for 1984. Aluminium body on separate steel chassis. Body has higher tail than the tapering back of the saloon.

Engine: Front-mounted V8-cylinder with twin ohc for each bank; all alloy construction. 4-choke Weber carb. Bore 100 mm, stroke 85 mm; capacity 5341 cc. No power or torque figures quoted by Aston Martin, but power output probably around 300 bhp. Compression 9.3-to-1.

Transmission: Rear-wheel drive; five-speed manual gearbox; Torqueflite automatic transmission available. Limited slip diff. Top gear speed at 1000 rpm: 26.0 mph (41.8 km/h).

Suspension: Front, independent, wishbones and coil springs; telescopic dampers. Anti-roll bar. Rear, De Dion axle with Watts linkage and longitudinal arms. Coil springs and adjustable telescopic dampers.

Steering: Rack and pinion. Power assistance: standard.

Brakes: Vented discs front and rear, servo-assisted.

Tyres: GR 70 VR 15.   **Fuel tank:** 23 Imp. gall (105 litres).

Dimensions: Length 183.7 in (4665 mm), width 72 in (1830 mm), height 52 in (1325 mm), wheelbase 103 in (2610 mm).

Unladen weight: 3924 lb (1780 kg).

Performance *Autocar* test: Maximum speed 146 mph (235 km/h); 0 to 60 mph (100 km/h) 6.6 sec. Fuel consumption at constant 75 mph (120 km/h), 18.4 mpg, overall test, 14.0 mpg.

Features: Improved air conditioning, Blaupunkt radio and BBS wheels introduced 1984. Rather noisy but magnificent response and a most rewarding and satisfying car to drive. Superb equipment and finish with leather upholstery and polished walnut veneer trim.

Identity: In keeping with their plan to offer four-wheel drive on every model, Audi continue with the Quattro version of the 80, though all 80s for 1985 have four-cylinder engines.

Engine: Front-mounted in-line four-cylinder with Bosch K-Jetronic fuel injection. Belt-driven ohc. Alloy head. Bore 81 mm, stroke 86.4 mm; capacity 1781 cc. Power 112 bhp (84 kW) at 5800 rpm; torque 109 lb ft (151 Nm) at 3500 rpm. Compression 10.0-to-1.

Transmission: Four-wheel drive; five-speed manual gearbox; Centre and rear diffs. lockable for extreme conditions. Top gear speed at 1000 rpm: 20.3 mph (32.7 km/h).

Suspension: Front, independent, MacPherson struts and coil springs; telescopic dampers. Anti-roll bar. Rear, dead beam torsion axle on trailing arms and MacPherson struts with Panhard rod; coil springs; telescopic dampers. Anti-roll bar.

Steering: Rack and pinion. Power assistance: standard.

Brakes: Discs front and rear, servo-assisted.

Tyres: 175/70 HR 14.   **Fuel tank:** 15.4 Imp. gall (70 litres).

Dimensions: Length 172.6 in (4385 mm), width 66.2 in (1681 mm), height 54.1 in (1375 mm), wheelbase 99.4 in (2525 mm).

Unladen weight: 2557 lb (1160 kg).

Performance *Autocar* test: Maximum speed 114 mph (184 km/h); 0 to 60 mph (100 km/h) 9.2 sec. Fuel consumption at constant 75 mph (120 km/h): 34.9 mpg.

Features: Good compromise on performance, price and equipment, where the paramount need is to have the four-wheel drive facility. But if the budget allows, the additional performance and refinement of the five-cylinder engine will tempt one to the 90.

Identity: Realigned Audi range announced September 1984 brought a new model—the 90, with five-cylinder engine, fuel injection and CD trim. Four-wheel drive also available, in the 90 Quattro. UK versions have 2.2-litre engine, but some other markets also have 2-litre Audi 90.

Engine: Front-mounted in-line five-cylinder with Bosch K-Jetronic fuel injection. Belt-driven ohc. Electronic ignition. Bore 81.0 mm, stroke 86.4 mm; capacity 2226 cc. Power 136 bhp (100 kW) at 5700 rpm; torque 135 lb ft (186 Nm) at 3500 rpm. Compression 10.0-to-1.

Transmission: Front-wheel drive; five-speed manual gearbox; automatic transmission optional for two-wheel drive model. Top gear speed at 1000 rpm: 21.6 mph (34.8 km/h).

Suspension: Front, independent, MacPherson struts and coil springs; telescopic dampers. Anti-roll bar. Rear, dead beam torsion axle on trailing arms and MacPherson struts with Panhard rod; coil springs and telescopic dampers. Anti-roll bar.

Steering: Rack and pinion. Power assistance: standard.

Brakes: Discs front and rear, servo-assisted. Anti-lock optional.

Tyres: 185/60 HR 14.   **Fuel tank:** 15.4 Imp. gall (70 litres).

Dimensions: Length 175.8 in (4465 mm), width 66 in (1682 mm), height 54 in (1376 mm), wheelbase 99.4 in (2525 mm).

Unladen weight: 2645 lb (1200 kg).

Performance *Autocar* test: Maximum speed 124 mph (200 km/h); 0 to 60 mph (100 km/h) 9.0 sec. Fuel consumption at constant 75 mph (120 km/h): 31.0 mpg.

Features: Refined and comfortable car with good handling, excellent engine response, and high level of standard equipment. Neat interior trim, with velour upholstery. Wide range of extras available.

AUDI (D)   100 Turbo Diesel

Identity: Extraordinary combination of space, refinement and economy. Big tank gives huge range, as I demonstrated in July 1984, setting a world record for longest distance in a standard car without refuelling: Land's End to John o' Groats, and then back nearly to Glasgow—total 1,150.3 miles at 51.1 mph average and 59.3 mpg overall.

Engine: Front-mounted in-line five-cylinder with belt-driven single ohc. Indirect injection, and turbocharger. Bore 76.5 mm, stroke 86.4 mm; capacity 1986 cc. Power 87 bhp (64 kW) at 4500 rpm; torque 127 lb ft (175 Nm) at 2750 rpm. Compression 23.0-to-1.

Transmission: Front-wheel drive; five-speed manual gearbox; three-speed automatic transmission optional. Top gear speed at 1000 rpm: 26.8 mph (43.1 km/h).

Suspension: Front, independent, MacPherson struts and coil springs; telescopic dampers. Anti-roll bar. Rear, semi-independent, dead beam torsion axle on trailing arms with Panhard rod; coil springs and telescopic dampers. Torsion beam gives anti-roll effect.

Steering: Rack and pinion. Power assistance: standard.

Brakes: Discs front drums rear, hydraulic servo-assisted.

Tyres: 185/70 SR 14.   **Fuel tank:** 17.6 Imp. gall (80 litres).

Dimensions: Length 188.7 in (4793 mm), width 71.4 in (1814 mm), height 56.0 in (1422 mm), wheelbase 105.8 in (2687 mm).

Unladen weight: 2756 lb (1250 kg).

Performance (Works): Maximum speed 108 mph (174 km/h); 0 to 60 mph (100 km/h) 14.0 sec. Fuel consumption at constant 75 mph (120 km/h): 37.2 mpg.

Features: Picture shows the Audi actually on that run to establish record range, heading north on M6. Quite well equipped car.

AUDI (D)   200 Quattro Avant

Identity: In line with Audi's prediction that all their models would eventually be offered with four-wheel drive, a hatchback estate version of the 200 Quattro Turbo was launched Paris 1984. Mechanically as saloon version, this must rate as the fastest load carrier on the road.

Engine: Front-mounted in-line five-cylinder with belt-driven ohc; alloy head. KKK turbocharger with inter-cooler and knock sensor. Bore 79.5 mm, stroke 86.4 mm; capacity 2144 cc. Power 182 bhp (134 kW) at 5700 rpm; torque 182 lb ft (252 Nm) at 3600 rpm. Comp. 8.8-to-1.

Transmission: Four-wheel drive; five-speed manual gearbox; automatic transmission optional. Top gear speed at 1000 rpm: 23.6 mph (37.9 km/h). Lockable front and rear diffs.

Suspension: Front, independent, MacPherson struts and coil springs; telescopic dampers. Anti-roll bar. Rear, independent, with four-joint trapezoidal arms and coil springs; telescopic dampers (new rear layout autumn 1984).

Steering: Rack and pinion. Power assistance: standard.

Brakes: Vented discs front, solid discs rear, servo-assisted. Anti-lock standard.

Tyres: 205/60 VR 15.   **Fuel tank:** 17.6 Imp. gall (80 litres).

Dimensions: Length 188.7 in (4793 mm), width 71.4 in (1814 mm), height 56 in (1422 mm), wheelbase 105.8 in (2687 mm).

Unladen weight: 3108 lb (1410 kg).

Performance (Works): Maximum speed 139 mph (224 km/h); 0 to 60 mph (100 km/h) 8.2 sec. Fuel consumption at constant 75 mph (120 km/h): 29.4 mpg.

Features: Superbly equipped with such refinements as anti-lock brakes (ABS) standard, in addition to the more usual items such as electric window lifts with semi-automatic function, and central locking.

AUSTIN (GB)   Metro 1.3 HLE 5-door

Identity: Originally introduced Birmingham 1982, and the same Motor Show two years later brought introduction of the new 5-door Metro. New instrument layout, similar to Montego, and revised front giving better air flow.

Engine: Front-mounted transverse four-cylinder with pushrod ohv. Cast iron head and block. Bore 70.6 mm, stroke 81.3 mm; capacity 1275 1275 cc. Power 60 bhp (45 kW) at 5250 rpm; torque 69 lb ft (95 Nm) at 3200 rpm. Compression 9.4-to-1.

Transmission: Front-wheel drive; four-speed manual gearbox; Automatic transmission available in one specific model. Top gear speed at 1000 rpm: 17.2 mph (26.7 km/h).

Suspension: Front, independent, unequal length links; bottom link braced by anti-roll bar. Hydragas springs and integral dampers. Rear, independent, connected side to side, trailing arms. Hydragas springs with coil springs pre-load. Internal damping in Hydragas strut.

Steering: Rack and pinion. Power assistance: not available.

Brakes: Discs front, drums rear, servo-assisted.

Tyres: 155/70-12.   **Fuel tank:** 7.8 Imp. gall (35.4 litres).

Dimensions: Length 134 in (3405 mm), width 60.9 in (1549 mm), height 53.6 in (1361 mm), wheelbase 88.6 in (2251 mm).

Unladen weight: 1820 lb (840 kg).

Performance (Works): Maximum speed 95 mph (152 km/h); 0 to 60 mph (100 km/h) 13.5 sec. Fuel consumption at constant 75 mph (120 km/h): 39.5 mpg.

Features: New 5-door body increases the appeal of the Metro range. Interior specification raised with Montego instrumentation. Larger fuel tank an improvement, and equipment generally more generous.

23

AUSTIN (GB)   Montego 2.0L Estate car

Identity: Additions to the Montego range at Birmingham 1984 were five estate car models with generous 60 cu ft carrying capacity. Available with either the 1.6- or 2.0-litre engine. 1.6 has four-speed gearbox, 2.0 gets five-speed, which is also optional for 1.6. Automatic available for 1.6 only.

Engine: Front-mounted transverse four-cylinder with programmed electronic ignition and engine management systems. Bore 84.5 mm, stroke 89 mm; capacity 1994 cc. Power 102 bhp (76 kW) at 5500 rpm; torque 121 lb ft (167 Nm) at 3000 rpm. Compression 9.1-to-1.

Transmission: Front-wheel drive; five-speed manual gearbox; automatic transmission optional for 1.6L and HL. Top gear speed at 1000 rpm: 26.8 mph (43.2 km/h).

Suspension: Front, independent, MacPherson struts and lower arms, coil springs; telescopic dampers. Anti-roll bar. Rear, 'H-frame' interconnected trailing arms, coil springs and telescopic dampers. Self-levelling rear suspension optional.

Steering: Rack and pinion. Power assistance: optional for 2-litre.

Brakes: Discs front, drums rear, servo-assisted.

Tyres: 180/65 R 365 TD.   **Fuel tank:** 11 Imp. gall (50 litres).

Dimensions: Length 175.9 in (4468 mm), width 67.3 in (1710 mm), height 57.0 in (1447 mm), wheelbase 101.2 in (2570 mm).

Unladen weight: 2350 lb (1065 kg).

Performance (Works): Maximum speed 108 mph (174 km/h); 0 to 60 mph (100 km/h) 10.2 sec. Fuel consumption at constant 75 mph (120 km/h): 37.3 mpg.

Features: Optional rearward-facing third row of seats; special roof rack with removable bars available. Concealed space for stowage out of view.

AUTOBIANCHI (I)   A112 Abarth

Identity: Small Italian car of sporting character, sadly not imported to Britain. Chunky, two-door hatchback body. Several versions of Autobianchi are available, starting with the Junior; Abarth is the performance model with tuned engine.

Engine: Front-mounted four-cylinder with alloy head, chain-driven side camshaft and pushrods. Weber twin-choke carb. Bore 67.2 mm; stroke 74 mm; capacity 1049 cc. Power, 69 bhp (51.5 kW) at 6000 rpm; torque 119 lb ft (86 Nm) at 4200 rpm. Compression 10.4-to-1.

Transmission: Front-wheel drive; four-speed gearbox standard; five-speed optional. Top gear speed at 1000 rpm: 16.8 mph (27.0 km/h).

Suspension: Front, independent, MacPherson struts and soil springs; telescopic dampers. Anti-roll bar. Rear, independent, wishbones and transverse leaf spring; telescopic dampers.

Steering: Rack and pinion. Power assistance: not available.

Brakes: Disc front, drums rear, servo-assisted.

Tyres: 155/70 SR 13.   **Fuel tank:** 6.6 Imp gall (30 litres).

Dimensions: Length 127 in (3230 mm), width 58 in (1480 mm), height 53.5 in (1360 mm), wheelbase 80.3 in (2040 mm).

Unladen weight: 1543 lb (700 kg).

Performance (Works): Maximum speed, 99 mph (159 km/h). 0 to 60 mph (100 km/h) 12.3 sec. Fuel consumption, 36.2 mpg at constant 75 mph (120 km/h).

Features: Slightly basic interior trim, but car is well engineered and has sporting appeal, with extra instruments and alloy wheels in this top version. Crisp handling and tidy steering.

Identity: Introduced August 1984 as the 'cut-price' sporting Bentley aimed firmly at the young businessman who wants to move up to such a car, probably for the first time. Mechanically based on the Mulsanne, the differences are a very slight lowering of equipment and the attractive new wire grille.

Engine: Front-mounted V8-cylinder with aluminium alloy construction, pushrod overhead valves with hydraulic tappets. Bore 104.1 mm, stroke 99.1 mm; capacity 6750 cc. No power or torque figures quoted by Rolls-Royce for their engines. Compression 9.0-to-1.

Transmission: Rear-wheel drive; GM Hydra-Matic automatic transmission with Rolls-Royce adaptions, electric column selector. Top gear speed at 1000 rpm: 26.2 mph (41.2 km/h).

Suspension: Front, independent, wishbones and coil springs, telescopic dampers. Anti-roll bar. Rear, independent, semi-trailing arms and coil springs, telescopic dampers. Automatic self-levelling. Anti-roll bar.

Steering: Rack and pinion. Power assistance: standard.

Brakes: Ventilated discs front, solid discs rear, servo-assisted.

Tyres: 235/70 HR 15.   **Fuel tank:** 23.5 Imp. gall (107 litres).

Dimensions: Length 248 in (5310 mm), width 74.4 in (1890 mm), height 59 in (1490 mm), wheelbase 120.5 in (3060 mm).

Unladen weight: 2270 lb (5005 kg).

Performance *Autocar* test of Silver Spirit: Maximum speed 119 mph (191 km/h); 0 to 60 mph (100 km/h) 10.0 sec. Fuel consumption at constant 75 mph (120 km/h): 16.1 mpg; overall test, 14.0 mpg.

Features: Despite being the bottom of the range, the Eight still offers the 'standard' Rolls-Royce quality and superb finish. For its role as the sporting model, this version has slightly stiffer suspension.

BITTER (D)   SC Coupé

Identity: Elegantly styled four-seater Coupé, also available as Convertible and with choice of 3.0- or 3.7-litre engine. Four-wheel drive available. Steel body; mechanical components taken from Opel Monza/Senator range. Bitter is Germany's smallest car firm. Saloon became available on UK market, Birmingham 1984.

Engine: Front-mounted in-line six-cylinder with chain-driven camshaft in head, and hydraulic tappets. Bosch L-Jetronic fuel injection. Bore 95 mm, stroke 69.8 mm; capacity 2968 cc. Power 170 bhp (127 kW at 5800 rpm; torque 173 lb ft (235 Nm) at 4500 rpm. Compression 9.4-to-1.

Transmission: Rear-wheel drive; five-speed manual gearbox; GM three-speed automatic transmission optional. Top gear speed at 1000 rpm: 23.5 mph (37.8 km/h). Power assistance to come.

Suspension: Front, independent, MacPherson struts; coil springs and telescopic dampers. Anti-roll bar. Rear, independent, semi-trailing arm, double conical miniblock coil springs and telescopic dampers. Anti-roll bar.

Steering: Recirculating ball; power assistance: standard.

Brakes: Vented discs front, solid discs rear, servo-assisted.

Tyres: 215/60 VR 15.   **Fuel tank:** 16 Imp. gall (73 litres).

Dimensions: Length 193.3 in (4910 mm), width 71.7 in (1820 mm), height 53 in (1350 mm), wheelbase 105.6 in (2683 mm).

Unladen weight: 3417 lb (1550 kg).

Performance (Works): Maximum speed 130 mph (209 km/h), 0 to 60 mph (100 km/h) 9.0 sec. Fuel consumption (est.) 24 mpg.

Features: Lavish equipment includes central locking, remote control mirrors, cruise control, cassette/radio.

BMW (D)   323i convertible

Identity: After construction at Munich, examples of the 3-Series two-door model are shipped to Baur coachbuilders for adaptation to convertible bodywork. Removable roof panel and folding rear quarter hood; fixed roll bar and side window frames. Conversion available for any 3-Series two-door model; top 323i details below.

Engine: Front-mounted in-line six-cylinder with belt-driven single ohc and inclined valves in hemi head. Bosch L-Jetronic injection. Bore 80 mm, stroke 76.8 mm; capacity 2316 cc. Power 139 bhp (102 kW) at 5300 rpm; torque 148 lb ft (205 Nm) at 4000 rpm. Compression 9.8-to-1.

Transmission: Rear-wheel drive; five-speed manual gearbox; three-speed automatic optional. Final drive 3.25-to-1. Top gear speed at 1000 rpm: 25.4 mph (40.9 km/h).

Suspension: Front, independent, MacPherson struts and coil springs; telescopic dampers. Anti-roll bar. Rear, independent, semi-trailing arms and coil springs; telescopic dampers. Anti-roll bar.

Steering: Rack and pinion. Power assistance: optional.

Brakes: Vented discs front, solid discs rear, servo-assisted.

Tyres: 195/60 VR 14.   **Fuel tank:** 12.1 Imp. gall (55 litres).

Dimensions: Length 170 in (4325 mm), width 64.8 in (1645 mm), height 54.3 in (1380 mm), wheelbase 101 in (2570 mm).

Unladen weight: 2380 lb (1080 kg).

Performance *Autocar* test saloon: Maximum speed 112 mph (180 km/h); 0 to 60 mph (100 km/h) 8.3 sec. Fuel consumption at constant 75 mph (120 km/h): 34.5 mpg; overall test, 23.1 mpg.

Features: Very pleasant when open, but some drawbacks in terms of reduced visibility to the rear, and extra noise. Roof panel when stowed in boot reduces boot access and space. Very neat finish.

Identity: Launched November 1984, and on British market January 1985, the four-cylinder version of 5-Series was given fuel injection for better power and economy; gearing slightly higher, and power steering became standard.

Engine: Front-mounted in-line four-cylinder with chain-driven ohc. Bosch L-Jetronic fuel injection. Bore 89 mm, stroke 71 mm; capacity 1766 cc. Power 105 bhp (77 kW) at 5800 rpm; torque 105 lb ft (145 Nm) at 4500 rpm. Compression 9.5-to-1.

Transmission: Rear-wheel drive; five-speed manual gearbox; no automatic transmission option. Final drive 4.10-to-1. Top gear speed at 1000 rpm: 21.1 mph (34.1 km/h).

Suspension: Front, independent, MacPherson struts and double links; coil springs and telescopic dampers. Anti-roll bar. Rear, independent, semi-trailing arms and coil springs; telescopic dampers.

Steering: Gemmer ball and nut. Power assistance: standard.

Brakes: Discs front, drums rear, servo-assisted.

Tyres: 175 TR 14.   **Fuel tank:** 15.4 Imp. gall (70 litres).

Dimensions: Length 182 in (4620 mm), width 67 in (1699 mm), height 55.7 in (1415 mm), wheelbase 103 in (2624 mm).

Unladen weight: 2513 lb (1140 kg).

Performance (Works): Maximum speed 109 mph (175 km/h); 0 to 60 mph (100 km/h) 12.6 sec. Fuel consumption at constant 75 mph (120 km/h): 35.3 mpg.

Features: Still very much a four-cylinder, and has to be worked fairly hard for good performance, but response appreciably better than with carburettor model. Well-finished and quite good equipment. Strong business appeal in Britain due to engine size.

BMW (D)

525eta

Identity: It has long been held that a big engine is not necessarily uneconomical, especially if it is geared suitably high, and is developed to give high torque at low revs. The BMW 525eta was the car launched mid-1983 which certainly proved this concept to be true. Sometimes it is known as simply 525e (eta is the Greek symbol for efficiency).

Engine: Front-mounted in-line six-cylinder with alloy head; belt-drive ohc. Motronic fuel injection and ignition system. Bore 84 mm, stroke 81 mm; capacity 2693 cc. Power 125 bhp (92 kW) at 4250 rpm; torque 177 lb ft (240 Nm) at 3250 rpm. Compression 11.0-to-1.

Transmission: Rear-wheel drive; five-speed manual gearbox; four speed automatic optional (standard in UK), with torque converter lock-up. Top gear speed at 1000 rpm: 33.6 mph (54.1 km/h).

Suspension: Front, independent, MacPherson struts and double links; coil springs and telescopic dampers. Anti-roll bar. Rear, independent semi-trailing arms; coil springs and telescopic dampers.

Steering: ZF ball and nut. Power assistance: standard.

Brakes: Discs front and rear, servo-assisted.

Tyres: 175 HR 14.   **Fuel tank:** 15.4 Imp. gall (70 litres).

Dimensions: Length 182 in (4620 mm), width 67 in (1699 mm), height 55.7 in (1415 mm), wheelbase 103 in (2624 mm).

Unladen weight: 2919 lb (1326 kg).

Performance *Autocar* test: Maximum speed 111 mph (179 km/h); 0 to 60 mph (100 km/h) 10.2 sec. Fuel consumption at constant 75 mph (120 km/h), 37.7 mpg; overall test 26.2 mpg.

Features: Very quiet and refined car, helped by exceptionally high gearing with high-torque engine. Well-finished, but rather a lot of extra money is needed to complete the specification with such items as sunroof, central locking and alloy wheels all extra.

BMW (D)   M535i

Identity: Fastest saloon BMW yet was launched November 1984—on UK market this January, as well as 518i. Developed by BMW Motorsport, it has the 3.43-litre engine in 5-Series body, with very high gearing, spoiler at rear, and front airdam. Look for M badge in blue/red Motorsport colours, and matching coachlines on sides.

Engine: Front-mounted in-line six-cylinder with chain-driven single ohc. Motronic control of fuel injection and ignition. Bore 92 mm, stroke 86 mm; capacity 3430 cc. Power 218 bhp (160 kW) at 5200 rpm; torque 224 lb ft (310 Nm) at 4000 rpm. Compression 10.0-to-1.

Transmission: Rear-wheel drive; five-speed manual gearbox; four-speed automatic with switchable Sport/Economy mode optional. Top gear speed at 1000 rpm: 29.0 mph (46.6 km/h).

Suspension: Front, independent, MacPherson struts and double links; coil springs and telescopic dampers. Anti-roll bar. Rear, independent, semi-trailing arms with wheel control links; coil springs and gas-filled telescopic dampers. Anti-roll bar.

Steering: Ball and nut. Power assistance: standard, effort varies according to speed.

Brakes: Vented discs front, solid discs rear, servo-assisted. Anti-lock standard.

Tyres: 220/55 VR 390 TRX.   **Fuel tank**: 15.4 Imp. gall (70 litres).

Dimensions: Length 181 in (4604 mm), width 67.3 in (1710 mm), height 55 in (1397 mm), wheelbase 103.5 in (2628 mm).

Unladen weight: 3064 lb (1390 kg).

Performance (Works): Maximum speed 143 mph (230 km/h); 0 to 60 mph (100 km/h) 7.2 sec. Fuel consumption at constant 75 mph (120 km/h): 31.4 mpg.

Features: Lavishly equipped, with anti-lock brakes, on-board computer, limited slip differential, and many other special items.

BMW (D)

Identity: Launched Frankfurt 1983, this is an additional version of the superb 635 Coupé, with the same high performance 24-valve engine as fitted in the M1. Few differences in outward appearance from ordinary 635, but look for the lower front spoiler and 'M' insignia.

Engine: Front-mounted in-line six-cylinder with twin ohc and four valves per cylinder. Alloy head. Digital electronics for injection/ignition. Bore 93.4 mm, stroke 84 mm; capacity 3453 cc. Power 282 bhp (210 kW) at 6500 rpm; torque 246 lb ft (340 Nm) at 4500 rpm. Compression 10.5-to-1.

Transmission: Rear-wheel drive; five-speed manual gearbox; no automatic option, and heavy duty sports gearbox is used. Top gear speed at 1000 rpm: 25.2 mph (40.6 km/h).

Suspension: Front, independent, MacPherson struts and double jointed links; coil springs and telescopic dampers. Anti-roll bar. Rear, independent, semi-trailing arms with wheel control links; coil springs and telescopic dampers. Anti-roll bar.

Steering: ZF ball and nut. Power assistance: standard.

Brakes: Vented discs front, solid rear, servo-assisted. ABS standard.

Tyres: TRX 220/55 VR 390.   **Fuel tank:** 15.4 Imp. gall (70 litres).

Dimensions: Length 187 in (4755 mm), width 68 in (1725 mm), height 53.3 in (1354 mm), wheelbase 103.3 in (2625 mm).

Unladen weight: 3307 lb (1500 kg).

Performance (Works): Maximum speed 159 mph (256 km/h); 0 to 60 mph (100 km/h) 6.4 sec. Fuel consumption at constant 75 mph (120 km/h) 27.7 mpg.

Features: Elaborate standard equipment. Reinforced and enlarged front disc brakes. M-style wheels.

BMW (D)

Identity: In Britain, this is the top model of the 7-Series BMW range, though in Germany there is also the 745i, with turbocharged engine. Detail improvements announced October 1982 include revised radiator grille and electric driving seat adjustment with 'memory'. Automatic model is switchable—Sport or Economy, to suit style of driving.

Engine: Front-mounted six-cylinder with chain-driven single ohc. Alloy head. Bore 92 mm, stroke 86 mm; capacity 3430 cc. Power, 218 bhp (163 kW) at 5200 rpm; torque 224 lb ft. (310 Nm) at 4000 rpm. Compression 10-to-1.

Transmission: Rear-wheel drive; five-speed manual gearbox or four-speed automatic, with anti-slip torque converter brake. Top gear speed at 1000 rpm: 33.1 mph (53.3 km/h).

Suspension: Front, independent, MacPherson struts; coil springs and telescopic dampers. Anti-roll bar. Rear, independent, semi-trailing arms with extra wheel-control linkages as 528i. Coil springs and telescopic dampers.

Steering: ZF ball and nut; Power assistance: standard.

Brakes: Vented discs front, solid discs rear, servo-assisted.

Tyres: 205/70 HR 14.   **Fuel tank:** 22 Imp. gall (100 litres).

Dimensions: Length 191.3 in (4859 mm), width 70.9 in (1801 mm), height 56.3 in (1430 mm), wheelbase 110 in (2794 mm).

Unladen weight: 3374 lb (1530 kg).

Performance (Works): Maximum speed, 132 mph (212 km/h). 0 to 60 mph (100 km/h) 7.7 sec. Fuel consumption, 28.8 mpg at constant 75 mph (120 km/h).

Features: Superbly finished and lavishly equipped car in new and even more refined form. Advanced automatic transmission.

BRISTOL (GB)   Beaufighter convertible

Identity: Hand-built and very exclusive car; the cabriolet version of this Bristol was introduced January 1980. Impressive performance with turbocharged engine.

Engine: Front-mounted V8-cylinder with Carter carburettor and turbocharger. Bore 101.6 mm, stroke 91 mm; capacity 5898 cc. Power and torque figures not quoted by manufacturer.

Transmission: Rear-wheel drive; Chrysler Torqueflite automatic transmission standard; manual transmission not available. Top gear speed at 1000 rpm: 26 mph (42 km/h).

Suspension: Front, independent, wishbones and coil springs, telescopic dampers. Anti-roll bar. Rear, live axle on longitudinal links, Watts linkage, torsion bars.

Steering: Recirculating ball. Power assistance: standard.

Brakes: Discs front and rear, servo-assisted.

Tyres: 225/70-15.   **Fuel tank:** 18 Imp. gall (82 litres).

Dimensions: Length 194.5 in (4940 mm), width 69.5 in (1765 mm); height 57 in (1447 mm), wheelbase 114 in (2895 mm).

Unladen weight: 3858 lb (1750 kg).

Performance (Works): Maximum speed 140 mph (225 km.h); 0 to 60 mph (100 km/h) 7.0 sec. Fuel consumption: 15.7 mpg (touring).

Features: The turbocharged Chrysler V8 engine makes the Beaufighter an impressively fast car. Well-engineered if rather ponderous. Aluminium body was designed by Zagato. A high price tag for this car, but accompanying high level of luxury.

BRISTOL (GB)   Beaufort turbo convertible

Identity: Addition to Bristol range at Birmingham 1984 was the Beaufort, reviving famous Bristol aircraft name. Based on Beaufighter, but with true convertible body, having no roll-over bars when hood lowered. Production in left-drive, for export only. Despite similar appearance, many panels changed.

Engine: Front-mounted Chrysler V8-cylinder with hydraulic tappets, Carter carburettor and turbocharger. Bore 101.6 mm, stroke 91 mm; capacity 5898 cc. No data on power and torque revealed by Bristol. Compression 8.5-to-1.

Transmission: Rear-wheel drive; Chrysler Torqueflite automatic transmission; no manual transmission option. Top gear speed at 1000 rpm: 26.0 mph (41.8 km/h).

Suspension: Front, independent, wishbones and coil springs; telescopic dampers. Anti-roll bar. Rear, live-axle on longitudinal links with Watts linkage and torsion bars; telescopic dampers with self-levelling provision.

Steering: Recirculating ball. Power assistance: standard.

Brakes: Discs front and rear, servo-assisted.

Tyres: 225/70 VR 15.   **Fuel tank:** 28 Imp. gall (127 litres).

Dimensions: Length 194.5 in (4940 mm), width 68.5 in (1740 mm), height 57 in (1447 mm), wheelbase 114 in (2895 mm).

Unladen weight: 3850 lb (1746 kg).

Performance (Works): Maximum speed 150 mph (242 km/h); 0 to 60 mph (100 km/h) 6.0 sec. Fuel consumption at constant 75 mph (120 km/h): 16.0 mpg.

Features: Four-seater touring convertible with electric operation for hood. Leather upholstery. Only 150 Bristols are built each year.

BUICK (USA)   Century Limited Sedan

Identity: The front-wheel drive Century range include a Custom Coupé, Sedan, Wagon, Limited Coupé and Sedan, Estate and T Type Coupé. The latter has Bosch fuel injection and three-speed automatic transmission. Range has variety of engine options.

Engine: Front-mounted V6-cylinder with Bosch electronic fuel injection. Bore 96.5 mm, stroke 86.4 mm; capacity 3791 cc. Power 125 bhp (93.5 kW) at 4400 rpm; torque 195 lb ft (265 Nm) at 2000 rpm. Compression 8.0-to-1.

Transmission: Front-wheel drive; three-speed automatic. Four-speed automatic available on some versions. Top gear speed at 1000 rpm: 37.7 mph (60.7 km/h).

Suspension: Front, independent, MacPherson struts, coil springs and telescopic dampers. Anti-roll bar. Rear, live axle on longitudinal links with Panhard rod. Coil springs and telescopic dampers.

Steering: Rack and pinion. Power assistance: standard.

Brakes: Discs front, drums rear, servo-assisted.

Tyres: 185/75-14.   **Fuel tank:** 13 Imp. gall (59 litres).

Dimensions: Length 190.9 in (4850 mm), width 67.7 in (1720 mm), height 54.1 in (1375 mm), wheelbase 104.9 in (2665 mm).

Unladen weight: 2899 lb (1315 kg) four-door.

Performance (Works): Maximum speed 108 mph (175 km/h). Fuel consumption: 23 mpg (est.).

Features: The T type is the sporting version of the Buick Century range and has bucket seats, leather sports steering wheel and comprehensive instrumentation.

BUICK (USA)   LeSabre

Identity: The big family model from Buick continues for 1985 in a range that includes two- and four-door sedans in Custom and Limited trim and two rear-wheel drive Wagons, the Le Sabre Estate and Electra Estate. Both Wagons have the 5.0-litre engine as standard; for the Sedans, a 3.8-litre V6 or a 5.7-litre diesel engine is available.

Engine: Front-mounted V8-cylinder with four-barrel carburettor. Bore 96.5 mm, stroke 85.9 mm; capacity 5033 cc. Power 140 bhp (104.5 kW) at 3600 rpm; torque 240.3 lb ft (326 Nm) at 1600 rpm. Compression 8-to-1.

Transmission: Rear-wheel drive; four-speed automatic transmission. Top gear speed at 1000 rpm: 42.6 mph (68.7 km/h).

Suspension: Front, independent, wishbones and coil springs; telescopic dampers. Anti-roll bar. Rear, live axle on longitudinal links with upper links on to diff. coil springs and telescopic dampers. Optional anti-roll bar.

Steering: Recirculating ball. Power assistance: standard.

Brakes: Ventilated discs front, drums rear, servo-assisted.

Tyres: 215/75 R 15.   **Fuel tank:** 20.9 Imp. gall (95 litres).

Dimensions: Length 218.5 in (5550 mm), width 76 in (1930 mm), height 56.7 in (1440 mm), wheelbase 115.9 in (2945 mm).

Unladen weight: 3726 lb (1690 kg).

Performance (Est.): Maximum speed 99 mph (160 km/h). Fuel consumption: 17 mpg (est.).

Features: Perimeter frame chassis. Six-passenger seating available in many versions of the LeSabre, while the Wagon variants can seat up to eight passengers.

BUICK (USA)   Regal Limited Coupé

Identity: The Regal was the best-selling Buick throughout 1984. Available as a two-door coupé, the Regal and Regal Limited, plus the performance versions—T Type and the Grand National. The four-door Regal has been discontinued. A new grille and different wheel covers have been introduced. Mechanically similar to last year's model.

Engine: Front-mounted V6-cylinder with hydraulic tappets. T Type and Grand National are fitted with a Garrett turbocharger. Bore 96.5 mm, stroke 86.3 mm; capacity 3791 cc. Power 110 bhp (82.5 kW) at 3800 rpm; torque 187 lb ft (258 Nm) at 1600 rpm. Compression 8.0-to-1.

Transmission: Rear-wheel drive; three-speed automatic transmission. Four-speed automatic available on T Type and Grand National. Top gear speed at 1000 rpm: 23.3 mph (37.5 km/h).

Suspension: Front, independent, wishbones and coil springs, telescopic dampers. Anti-roll bar. Rear, live axle on longitudinal arms, and links on to top of diff. Coil springs. Optional rear anti-roll bar.

Steering: Recirculating ball. Power assistance: standard.

Brakes: Discs front, drums rear, servo-assisted.

Tyres: 195/75-14.   **Fuel tank:** 15.2 Imp. gall (69 litres).

Dimensions: Length 200.6 in (5095 mm), width 71.5 in (1815 mm), height 54.3 in (1380 mm), wheelbase 108 in (2745 mm).

Unladen weight: 3252 lb (1475 kg).

Performance (Works): Maximum speed 93 mph (150 km/h). Fuel consumption: 19 mpg (est.).

Features: The Regal and Regal Limited are also available with a 4.3-litre V6 diesel engine. Woodgrain interior trim on the Regal Limited. The T Type gets new hydraulically-boosted brakes.

BUICK (USA)   Skyhawk

Identity: The smaller, compact front-wheel drive Buick. For 1985, available only as Custom or Limited Sedan; the coupé version has been dropped. New exterior colours, grille and tail-light assembly.

Engine: Front-mounted transverse four-cylinder with single belt drive ohc. Bore 101.6 mm, stroke 76.2 mm; capacity 2471 cc. Power 92 bhp (68.5 kW) at 4000 rpm; torque 131.9 lb ft (179 Nm) at 2800 rpm. Compression 8.2-to-1.

Transmission: Front-wheel drive; four-speed manual gearbox; or three-speed automatic. Top gear speed at 1000 rpm: 21.3 mph (34.4 km/h).

Suspension: Front, independent, MacPherson struts, coil springs and telescopic dampers. Anti-roll bar. Rear, dead beam axle on trailing arms and torsion beam, coil springs and telescopic dampers. Optional anti-roll bar.

Steering: Rack and pinion. Power assistance: standard.

Brakes: Discs front, drums rear, servo-assisted.

Tyres: 205/70-13.   **Fuel tank:** 12.1 Imp. gall (55 litres).

Dimensions: Length 181.1 in (4600 mm), width 68.9 in (1750 mm), height 53.7 in (1365 mm), wheelbase 104.9 in (2665 mm).

Unladen weight: 2557.4 lb (1160 kg).

Performance (Works): Maximum speed 95 mph (155 km/h). Fuel consumption: 24 mph (est.).

Features: While the standard engine is the four-cylinder 2.5-litre, a carburettor 2.8-litre V6 with four-speed manual or three-speed automatic is available. The Skyhawk has a new hydraulic engine mount system to dampen vibration.

CADILLAC (USA)   Cimarron

Identity: The compact model in the Cadillac range, first introduced April 1981. Available only as a four-door sedan, with optional luggage grid on the boot, and front-wheel drive.

Engine: Front-mounted four-cylinder with side camshaft and hydraulic tappets. Electronic fuel injection. Bore 92 mm, stroke 74 mm; capacity 1991 cc. Power 88 bhp (65.5 kW) at 4800 rpm; torque 109.8 lb ft (149 Nm) at 2400 rpm. Compression 8.5-to-1.

Transmission: Front-wheel drive; five-speed manual gearbox; three-speed automatic optional. Top gear speed at 1000 rpm: 24 mph (38.6 km/h).

Suspension: Front, independent, MacPherson struts, coil springs and telescopic dampers. Anti-roll bar. Rear, independent, semi-trailing arms and coil springs; telescopic dampers. Anti-roll bar.

Steering: Rack and pinion. Power assistance: standard.

Brakes: Discs front, drums rear, servo-assisted.

Tyres: 195/70 R-13.   **Fuel tank:** 11.3 Imp. gall (51.5 litres).

Dimensions: Length 173.2 in (4400 mm), width 66.3 in (1685 mm), height 51.9 in (1320 mm), wheelbase 101.2 in (2570 mm).

Unladen weight: 2579 lb (1170 kg).

Performance (Works): Maximum speed 93 mph (150 km/h). Fuel consumption: 24 mpg (est.).

Features: Very much the baby of the Cadillac range, from the General Motors J-car family. The Cimarron has less of the standard luxury features of other Cadillac models.

CADILLAC (USA) Eldorado Biarritz convertible

Identity: Introduced in the autumn of 1983, the Eldorado Biarritz convertible was the first open-topped Cadillac since 1976. A full five-seater, it has two-door body with power-operated vinyl roof and fixed glass rear window. A new vertical-accented grille distinguishes the 1985 model.

Engine: Front-mounted V8-cylinder with iron/alloy block. Electrical-mechanical digital fuel injection system. Bore 88 mm, stroke 84 mm; capacity 4087 cc. Power 135 bhp (101 kW) at 4400 rpm; torque 200 lb ft (271 Nm) at 2200 rpm. Compression 8.5-to-1.

Transmission: Front-wheel drive; three-speed Hydra-Matic transmission with overdrive. Column selector. Top gear speed at 1000 rpm: 25.2 mph (40.6 km/h).

Suspension: Front, independent, wishbones and longitudinal torsion bars. Telescopic dampers. Anti-roll bar. Rear, independent, semi-trailing arms and coil springs. Telescopic dampers. Anti-roll bar. Self-levelling provision.

Steering: Recirculating ball. Power assistance: standard.

Brakes: Discs front and rear, servo-assisted.

Tyres: 225/70 R 15.   **Fuel tank:** 16.9 Imp. gall (77 litres).

Dimensions: Length 204.5 in (5195 mm), width 71.5 in (1815 mm), height 54.3 in (1380 mm), wheelbase 113.9 in (2895 mm).

Unladen weight: 3913 lb (1775 kg).

Performance (Works): Maximum speed 90 mph (145 km/h).

Features: High level of interior trim, including leather seats and leather-trimmed steering wheel. Anti-theft system standard. New spoked aluminium-alloy wheels available for 1985.

CADILLAC (USA)   Seville Cabriolet

Identity: The imposing Cadillac Seville was first introduced in this form in 1980. For 1985 this distinctive overall design continues with the new vertical front grille and 'Cadillac' name badge. Available as four-door sedan, or cabriolet version.

Engine: Front-mounted V8-cylinder with iron/alloy block. Digital fuel injection system. Bore 88 mm, stroke 84 mm; capacity 4087 cc. Power 135 bhp (101 kW) at 4400 rpm; torque 200 lb ft (271 Nm) at 2200 rpm. Compression 8.5-to-1.

Transmission: Front-wheel drive; three-speed Hydra-Matic transmission with overdrive. Top gear speed at 1000 rpm: 37.8 mph (60.9 km/h).

Suspension: Front, independent, wishbones and longitudinal torsion bars; telescopic dampers. Anti-roll bar. Rear, independent, semi-trailing arms and coils springs; telescopic dampers. Anti-roll bar.

Steering: Recirculating ball. Power assistance: standard.

Brakes: Ventilated discs front, solid discs rear, servo-assisted.

Tyres: 205/75 R-15.   **Fuel tank:** 20.3 Imp. gall (76.8 litres).

Dimensions: Length 204.8 in (5202 mm), width 70.9 in (1801 mm), height 54.3 in (1379 mm), wheelbase 114.0 in (2895 mm).

Unladen weight: 3803 lb (1725 kg).

Performance (Works): Maximum speed 103 mph (175 km/h). Fuel consumption: 19 mpg (est.).

Features: A digital instrument panel cluster is available as an option on all Sevilles, as are leather seats. The door trims incorporate embroidered 'Seville' script.

CATERHAM CARS (GB)　　　Super Seven

Identity: Originally the Lotus Super Seven, but Caterham Cars of Surrey, England, took over the manufacturing rights, and the little two-seater sports car lives on in three forms: TC, GT, and GT Sprint. Decidedly basic weather protection, but tremendous fun.

Engine: Front-mounted four-cylinder with twin ohc. Two Dellorto carbs. Bore 81.0 mm, stroke 77.6 mm; capacity 1599 cc. Power, 120 bhp (90 kW) at 6300 rpm; torque 107 lb ft (148 Nm) at 5300 rpm. Compression 10.3-to-1.

Transmission: Rear-wheel drive; four-speed close ratio gearbox, with short travel change. Final drive 3.64-to-1. Top gear speed at 1000 rpm: 18.6 mph (29.9 km/h).

Suspension: Front, independent, wishbones and coil springs; telescopic dampers. Anti-roll bar. Rear, live axle on A-bracket, with trailing arms; coil springs and telescopic dampers.

Steering: Rack and pinion; Power assistance: not available.

Brakes: Discs front, drums rear, servo-assisted.

Tyres: 165 HR 13.　　　**Fuel tank:** 7.9 Imp. gall (36 litres).

Dimensions: Length 134 in (3403 mm), width 62.5 in (1587 mm), height 43.5 in (1104 mm), wheelbase 88 in (2235 mm).

Unladen weight: 1162 lb (527 kg).

Performance *Autocar* test: Maximum speed, 114 mph (184 km/h). 0 to 60 mph (100 km/h) 6.2 sec. Fuel consumption, 28.3 mph (overall).

Features: Terrific performance. Very direct steering and phenomenal roadholding. Detachable sidescreens and button-on hood. The nearest thing to a motor cycle with four wheels.

CHEVROLET (USA)　　　Camaro Z28

Identity: This sporting Chevrolet gets engine, suspension and cosmetic changes for 1985. Top of the list is a new model the Camaro IROC-Z, which takes its name from the cars specially prepared for America's International Race of Champions and powered by 5.0-litre engine in either carburettor or fuel injection form.

Engine: Front-mounted V8-cylinder with tuned port induction and Bosch fuel injection. Bore 94.9 mm, stroke 88.4 mm; capacity 5001 cc. Power 215 bhp (160 kW) at 4400 rpm; torque 275 lb ft (373 Nm) at 3200 rpm. Compression 9.5-to-1.

Transmission: Rear-wheel drive; four-speed automatic transmission with overdrive. Manual transmission available with carburettor'd version of 5.0 litre engine.

Suspension: Front, independent, wishbones and coil springs. Telescopic dampers. Anti-roll bar. Rear, live axles on semi-elliptic leaf springs; telescopic dampers. Anti-roll bar.

Steering: Recirculating ball. Power assistance: standard.

Brakes: Ventilated discs front and rear, servo-assisted.

Tyres: 215/65 R-15.　　**Fuel tank:** 13.1 Imp. gall (60 litres).

Dimensions: Length 187.8 in (4770 mm), width 72.8 in (1850 mm), height 50.0 in (1270 mm), wheelbase 100.9 in (2565 mm).

Unladen weight: 3439 lb (1560 kg).

Performance (Works): Maximum speed 130 mph (210 km/h). Fuel consumption: 18 mpg (est.).

Features: The famous Chevrolet Camaro Z28 has minor visual changes for 1985 including a deeper front spoiler, ground effect side skirts and revised rear bumper. There are a variety of engines with four, six or eight cylinders.

CHEVROLET (USA)

Cavalier Z24

Identity: The front-wheel drive J-car—the Cavalier— has been the best-selling car in America. The Cavalier range includes two-door hatchbacks and notchbacks, four-door sedans and wagons and a two-door convertible. Despite similar name, the American Cavalier has no direct relationship with the model available in Britain.

Engine: Front-mounted, transverse four-cylinder with hydraulic tappets and fuel injection. Bore 89 mm, stroke 80 mm; capacity 1991 cc. Power 88 bhp (66 kW) at 4800 rpm; torque 108 lb ft (149 Nm) at 2400 rpm. Compression 9.3-to-1.

Transmission: Front-wheel drive; four-speed manual gearbox; automatic or five-speed manual also available. Top gear speed at 1000 rpm: 25.8 mph (41.5 km/h).

Suspension: Front, independent, MacPherson struts; coil springs and telescopic dampers. Anti-roll bar. Rear, independent, semi-trailing arms, coil springs and telescopic dampers. Anti-roll bar optional.

Steering: Rack and pinion. Power assistance: standard.

Brakes: Ventilated discs front, drums rear, servo-assisted.

Tyres: 175/80 R 13.   Fuel tank: 11.7 Imp. gall (53 litres).

Dimensions: Length 170.9 in (4340 mm), width 66.4 in (1685 mm), height 53.9 in (1370 mm), wheelbase 101.2 in (2570 mm).

Unladen weight: 2359 lb (1070 kg).

Performance (est.): Maximum speed 102 mph (164 km/h). Fuel consumption: 18 mpg (est.).

Features: Power-operated hood and electric window lifts standard on convertible. Version illustrated, new for 1985, is a sporty Cavalier, the Z24. 125 bhp 2.8-litre V6 engine optional.

Identity: Now in its fourth year, the Celebrity was a move by Chevrolet towards a European styled car; but is still to be judged large by European standards. Wagon is available with either two or three rows of seating. All Celebrity models have 14 in. wheels for 1985.

Engine: Front-mounted transverse four-cylinder with hydraulic tappets. Fuel injection. V6 2.8 litre petrol and 4.3 litre diesel engines also available. Bore 101.6 mm, stroke 76.2 mm; capacity 2471 cc. Power 90 bhp (67 kW) at 4000 rpm; torque 134 lb ft (185 Nm) at 2400 rpm. Compression 8.3-to-1.

Transmission: Front-wheel drive; four-speed manual gearbox; three-speed automatic optional. Top gear speed at 1000 rpm: 25 mph (40.2 km/h).

Suspension: Front, independent, MacPherson struts; coil springs and telescopic dampers. Anti-roll bar. Rear, torsion beam axle on longitudinal links; Panhard rod, coil springs; telescopic dampers.

Steering: Rack and pinion. Power assistance: standard.

Brakes: Discs front, drums rear, servo-assisted.

Tyres: 205/70 R 14.   **Fuel tank:** 13 Imp. gall (59 litres).

Dimensions: Length 189 in (4800 mm), width 72.2 in (1783 mm), height 53.7 in (1365 mm), wheelbase 104.9 in (2665 mm).

Unladen weight: 2734 lb (1240 kg).

Performance (est.): Maximum speed 93 mph (150 km/h). Fuel consumption: 18 mpg (est.).

Features: Wide variety of options available, including a bench front seat, rear facing third row of seating and winding window for tailgate. Special Eurosport suspension package also available for 1985.

CHEVROLET (USA)   Corvette

Identity: The all-new Corvette was star of the Geneva Show in 1984. For its second year, the almost identical exterior conceals a number of mechanical changes, notably the new Tuned Port Injection 5.7-litre engine with a claimed 15 per cent performance boost.

Engine: Front-mounted V8-cylinder with Tuned Port Injection by Bosch. Bore 101.6 mm, stroke 88.4 mm; capacity 5736 cc. Power 230 bhp (171.5 kW) at 4000 rpm; torque 330 lb ft (448 Nm) at 3200 rpm. Compression 9.0-to-1.

Transmission: Rear-wheel drive; four-speed manual gearbox; with automatic overdrive on three upper gears.

Suspension: Front, independent, wishbones and tranverse glass fibre reinforced plastic leaf spring; telescopic dampers. Anti-roll bar. Rear, independent, five-link location; glass fibre reinforced (transverse) plastic leaf spring. Telescopic dampers. Anti-roll bar.

Steering: Rack and pinion. Power assistance: standard.

Brakes: Ventilated discs front and rear, servo-assisted.

Tyres: 215/65 R 15.   **Fuel tank:** 16.7 Imp. gall (76 litres).

Dimensions: Length 176.5 in (4483 mm), width 71.1 in (1805 mm), height 46.7 in (1185 mm), wheelbase 96 in (2438 mm).

Unladen weight: 3117 lb (1414 kg).

Performance *Autocar* test: Maximum speed 142 mph (228.5 km/h); 0 to 60 mph (100 km/h) 6.6 sec. Fuel consumption overall test, 16.7 mpg.

Features: The revival of a famous American sports car name has a number of interesting technical novelties. For 1985 the suspension has been softened, with now the same sized wheels—9.5 in. rims—on all four wheels (previous model had larger rear wheels).

CHEVROLET (USA)   Monte Carlo

Identity: Chevrolet's mid-range rear-wheel drive model available in two distinct forms. The Sedan has the fuel injected 4.3-litre V6 replacing last year's 3.8-litre engine, and the sporting SS with its 5.0-litre V8 available with two power outputs, 150 and 180 bhp (details here for larger engine).

Engine: Front-mounted 90 degree V8-cylinder with Rochester Quadrajet carburettor. Bore, 94.9 mm, stroke 88.4 mm; capacity 5001 cc. Power 180 bhp (134.5 kW) at 4800 rpm; torque 240 lb ft (326 Nm) at 3200 rpm. Compression 9.5-to-1.

Transmission: Rear-wheel drive; three- or four-speed automatic transmissions. Top gear speed at 1000 rpm: 29.9 mph (48.2 km/h).

Suspension: Front, independent, wishbones and coil springs; telescopic dampers. Anti-roll bar. Rear, live axle on longitudinal links, with upper links on to diff. Coil springs and telescopic dampers. Anti-roll bar.

Steering: Recirculating ball. Power assistance: standard.

Brakes: Ventilated discs front, drums rear, servo-assisted.

Tyres: 215/65 R 15.   **Fuel tank:** 15.1 Imp. gall (69 litres).

Dimensions: Length 220.4 in (5090 mm), width 71.8 in (1825 mm), height 54.3 in (1380 mm), wheelbase 108.1 in (2745 mm).

Unladen weight: 3262.8 lb (1480 kg).

Performance (est.): Maximum speed 125 mph (200 km/h). Fuel consumption: 18 mpg.

Features: The Monte Carlo SS is the road version of the American NASCAR-racing championship winning car. Previously available only in white or blue, colour options have been extended to include silver, maroon and black. Front seats are bucket for the SS, bench for the Sedan.

Identity: The big luxury saloon of the Chrysler range is the Fifth Avenue. Available only with 5.2-litre V8 engine and three-speed automatic, the model is described as a 'traditional luxury car'.

Engine: Front-mounted longitudinal V8-cylinder with chain-driven camshaft and hydraulic tappets. Twin-choke carb. Bore 99 mm, stroke 84 mm; capacity 5210 cc. Power 144 bhp (107 kW) at 3600 rpm; torque 265 lb ft (360 Nm) at 1600 rpm. Compression 9.0-to-1.

Transmission: Rear-wheel drive; three-speed Chrysler Torqflite automatic transmission. No manual version. Top gear speed at 1000 rpm: 34.7 mph (55.8 km/h).

Suspension: Front, independent, wishbones and transverse torsion bars; telescopic dampers. Anti-roll bar. Rear, live axle on semi-elliptic leaf springs; telescopic dampers.

Steering: Recirculating ball. Power assistance: standard.

Brakes: Discs front, drums rear, servo-assisted.

Tyres: P205/75 R 15.   **Fuel tank:** 15 Imp. gall (68 litres).

Dimensions: Length 206.7 in (5250 mm), width 74.2 in (1885 mm), height 55.3 in (1405 mm), wheelbase 112.7 in (2863 mm).

Unladen weight: 3690 lb (1674 kg).

Performance (est.): Maximum speed 105 mph (170 km/h). Fuel consumption: 17 mpg (est.).

Features: Very high level of standard specification, including automatic temperature control air conditioning, and electric windows. Additional luxury package available providing leather seats, wire wheels and 'heavy duty' rear suspension.

Identity: The Laser is claimed to be the first true Chrysler sports car. Front wheel drive with smooth, restrained 'European' styling in a two-door coupé body of good looks. There are two engine options: 2.2-litre fuel injected in either normally aspirated or turbocharged form.

Engine: Front-mounted transverse, four-cylinder with ohc, Bosch fuel injection, Garrett AiResearch turbocharged. Bore 87.4 mm, stroke 91.9 mm; capacity 2213 cc. Power 146 bhp (109 kW) at 5200 rpm; torque 168 lb ft (228 Nm) at 3600 rpm. Compression 8.1-to-1.

Transmission: Front-wheel drive; five-speed manual gearbox; standard, three-speed automatic optional. Top gear speed at 1000 rpm: 33.4 mph (53.8 km/h).

Suspension: Front, independent, MacPherson struts and coil springs; telescopic dampers. Anti-roll bar. Rear, trailing arms, coil springs; telescopic dampers. Anti-roll bar.

Steering: Rack and pinion. Power assistance: standard.

Brakes: Discs front, drums rear, servo-assisted.

Tyres: P195/70 R-14.   **Fuel tank:** 11.6 Imp. gall (53 litres).

Dimensions: Length 175 in (4445 mm), width 69.3 in (1760 mm), height 50.3 in (1278 mm), wheelbase 97.0 in (2464 mm).

Unladen weight: 2613 lb (1185 kg).

Performance (est.): Maximum speed 110 mph (180 km/h). Fuel consumption: 22 mpg (est.).

Features: Attractive new sports coupé from Chrysler. Available in two trim levels, the Laser XE having uprated suspension, low profile tyres and electronic instruments.

CHRYSLER (USA)   LeBaron convertible

Identity: There are four models in the LeBaron range: four-door sedan, two-door coupé, Town and Country Station Wagon, and Convertible. A 2.2-litre fuel injected engine is standard on all except the Station Wagon which has the 2.6-litre carburettor unit. A turbocharged 2.2-litre engine is an option on all models.

Engine: Front-mounted transverse four-cylinder with belt-driven single ohc and electronic fuel injection. Bore 87.4 mm, stroke 91.9 mm; capacity 2213 cc. Power 99 bhp (74 kW) at 5600 rpm; torque 121 lb ft (164 Nm) at 3200 rpm. Compression 9.0-to-1.

Transmission: Front-wheel drive; three-speed automatic transmission standard. Top gear speed at 1000 rpm: 31.5 mph (50.7 km/h).

Suspension: Front, independent, MacPherson struts and coil springs; telescopic dampers. Anti-roll bar. Rear, dead beam axle on trailing arms with Panhard rod, coil springs; telescopic dampers. Anti-roll bar.

Steering: Rack and pinion. Power assistance: standard.

Brakes: Discs front, drums rear, servo-assisted.

Tyres: 185/70 R-14.   **Fuel tank:** 10.8 Imp. gall (50 litres).

Dimensions: Length 179.8 in (4566 mm), width 67.9 (1725 mm), height 53.7 in (1364 mm), wheelbase 100.3 (2548 mm).

Unladen weight: 2616 lb (1187 kg).

Performance (est.): Maximum speed 105 mph (170 km/h). Fuel consumption: 25 mpg (est.).

Features: Fuel injection is new for 1985 on this model. Power-operated hood, tinted glass all round, rear compartment side windows. A luxury version offers leather seats and trimmings and electronic instruments.

CITROEN (F)   BX 19RD

Identity: First seen at the 1982 Paris Salon, the BX range gained two distinctly new models for 1985; a sporty GT version and an economical diesel-powered model. All models make extensive use of plastic materials for bonnet, rear hatch and some components.

Engine: Front-mounted transverse four-cylinder with camshaft in head, using glass fibre reinforced dog tooth drive. Bore 83 mm, stroke 88 mm; capacity 1905 cc. Power 65 bhp (48 kW) at 4600 rpm; torque 88.1 lb ft (119 Nm) at 2000 rpm. Compression 23.5-to-1.

Transmission: Front-wheel drive; five-speed manual gearbox; Top gear speed at 1000 rpm: 21.1 mph (34.0 km/h).

Suspension: Front, independent, wishbones and Citroen hydropneumatic units. Anti-roll bar. Rear, independent, trailing arms and Citroen hydropneumatic units. Automatic self levelling. Anti-roll bar.

Steering: Rack and pinion. Power assistance: not available.

Brakes: Discs front and rear, servo-assisted.

Tyres: 165/70 R-14.   **Fuel tank:** 11.4 Imp. gall (52 litres).

Dimensions: Length 166.5 in (4230 mm), width 65 in (1650 mm), height 53.6 in (1361 mm), wheelbase 104.5 in (2655 mm).

Unladen weight: 2072 lb (940 kg).

Performance *Autocar* test: Maximum speed 98 mph (158 km/h); 0 to 60 mph (100 km/h) 15.6 sec. Fuel consumption at constant 75 mph (120 km/h): 45.6 mpg; overall test, 42.1 mpg.

Features: Very stable and comfortable car, with the usual excellent Citroen ride. Diesel version has high level of specification including central locking, electric front window lifts and rear wash/wipe. A roomy and very economical five-seater.

Identity: Additions to Citroen BX range at Paris 1984 included introduction of four-speed automatic gearbox, and launch of a new 1.9-litre version called the GT. Look for GT badge on bonnet above headlamp, and twin foglamps beneath bumper.

Engine: Front-mounted transverse four-cylinder with belt-driven ohc. Engine inclined 30° rearwards. Bore 83 mm, stroke 88 mm; capacity 1905 cc. Power 101 bhp (75 kW) at 5600 rpm; torque 114 lb ft (158 Nm) at 3000 rpm. Compression 9.3-to-1.

Transmission: Front-wheel drive; five-speed manual gearbox; four-speed automatic option only for BX 16. Top gear speed at 1000 rpm: 21.0 mph (33.9 km/h).

Suspension: Front, independent, wishbones and Citroen Hydropneumatic units. Anti-roll bar. Rear, independent, trailing arms and Citroen Hydropneumatic units. Automatic self-levelling pressurized by engine-driven pump. Anti-roll bar.

Steering: Rack and pinion. Power assistance: standard.

Brakes: Discs front and rear, servo-assisted.

Tyres: 165/70 R 14.   **Fuel tank:** 11.4 Imp. gall (52 litres).

Dimensions: Length 166.5 in (4230 mm), width 65 in (1650 mm), height 53.6 in (1361 mm), wheelbase 104.5 in (2655 mm).

Unladen weight: 2072 lb (940 kg).

Performance (Works): Maximum speed 115 mph (185 km/h); 0 to 60 mph (100 km/h) 10.0 sec. Fuel consumption at constant 75 mph (120 km/h): 37.7 mpg.

Features: Comfort and stability of the BX are retained, with useful addition of extra performance and more relaxed cruising. Introduction of power-assisted steering also overcomes former criticism that the steering was too heavy. Well-equipped car; tweed upholstery.

CITROEN (F)   CX 25 GTI Turbo

Identity: Performance version of CX range, new at Paris 1984, was the GTI Turbo—one of the fastest Citroens ever produced, with top speed of 135 mph. Large spoiler on boot lid is chief recognition point. Citroen claim more performance without sacrificing economy.

Engine: Front-mounted transverse four-cylinder with Garrett T3 turbocharger. Chain-driven camshaft in block; pushrod valves. Bore 93 mm, stroke 92 mm; capacity 2500 cc. Power 164 bhp (122 kW) at 5000 rpm; torque 216 lb ft (299 Nm) at 3250 rpm. Comp. 7.75-to-1.

Transmission: Front-wheel drive; five-speed manual gearbox; no automatic option. Final drive 4.12-to-1. Top gear speed at 1000 rpm: 25.2 mph (40.5 km/h).

Suspension: Front, independent, double transverse arms, Citroen Hydropneumatic system with dampers in springs. Large diameter anti-roll bar. Rear, independent, trailing arms and Citroen Hydropneumatic units; larger diameter damper in discs in spring units. Anti-roll bar.

Steering: Rack and pinion. Power assistance: standard.

Brakes: Vented discs front, solid discs rear, servo-assisted.

Tyres: 210/55 VR 390.   **Fuel tank**: 15 Imp. gall (68 litres).

Dimensions: Length 183.5 in (4660 mm), width 69.7 in (1770 mm), height 53.5 in (1360 mm), wheelbase 112 in (2845 mm).

Unladen weight: 3053 lb (1385 kg).

Performance (Works): Maximum speed 135 mph (217 km/h); 0 to 60 mph (100 km/h) 8.0 sec. Fuel consumption at constant 75 mph (120 km/h): 28.5 mpg.

Features: Comprehensive equipment includes alloy wheels and full instrumentation in six round dials with analogue readouts. Leather upholstery and air conditioning optional.

CITROEN (F)   ECO 2000

Identity: Very much just a research vehicle, the ECO 2000 was one of the highlights of Paris 1984, and is included here as indication of Citroen's advanced work towards the practical economy car of the future. Drag coefficient is very low at 0.21.

Engine: Front-mounted transverse three-cylinder with water cooling; single overhead camshaft. Bore 70 mm, stroke 64.9 mm; capacity 750 cc. Power 35 bhp (25 kW) at 4750 rpm; torque 44 lb ft (61 Nm) at 2500 rpm. Compression 9.5-to-1.

Transmission: Front-wheel drive; four-speed manual gearbox; facia control and hydraulic operation. Top gear speed at 1000 rpm: 22.2 mph (35.7 km/h).

Suspension: Front, independent, MacPherson struts with Citroen Hydropneumatic units. Rear, independent, trailing arms and Citroen Hydropneumatic units. Map memory correction of vehicle attitude.

Steering: Rack and pinion. Power assistance: not envisaged.

Brakes: Discs front, drums rear, servo-assisted.

Tyres: Not determined, but rolling resistance to be reduced.

Dimensions: Length 137.4 in (3490 mm), width 58.4 in (1484 mm), height 50 in (1266 mm), wheelbase 89 in (2270 mm).

Unladen weight: 1058 lb (480 kg).

Performance (Works): Maximum speed 87 mph (140 km/h); 0 to 60 mph (100 km/h) 18 sec. Fuel consumption overall, 80 mpg (average of official figures).

Features: Programme started in 1981 with aim of achieving 90 mpg as average of official mpg figures. This was achieved in the two-cylinder versions. Ultra-smooth body shape and flush glass gives remarkably low wind resistance.

Identity: Last issue featured the Visa GT which was new at Paris 1982; since then has come (Paris 1984) the new TRS version of the Visa, taking its place between the 11RE and the GT. It has similar body and sporting looking wheels, but lacks the GT's side flash.

Engine: Front-mounted transverse four-cylinder with chain-driven ohc. Alloy block and head. Bore 75 mm, stroke 77 mm; capacity 1360 cc. Power 60 bhp (45 kW) at 5000 rpm; torque 77 lb ft (107 Nm) at 2500 rpm. Compression 9.3-to-1.

Transmission: Front-wheel drive; four-speed manual gearbox; five-speed optional (no automatic option). Top gear speed at 1000 rpm: 17.4 mph (28.1 km/h) in fourth.

Suspension: Front, independent, MacPherson struts and coil springs; telescopic dampers. Anti-roll bar. Rear, independent, trailing arms and coil springs; telescopic dampers.

Steering: Rack and pinion. Power assistance: not available.

Brakes: Discs front, drums rear, servo-assisted.

Tyres: 155/70 R 13.   **Fuel tank**: 8.8 Imp. gall (40 litres).

Dimensions: Length 146.4 in (3721 mm), width 60.5 in (1537 mm), height 55.8 in (1417 mm), wheelbase 95.3 in (2419 mm).

Unladen weight: 1764 lb (800 kg).

Performance (Works): Maximum speed 97 mph (156 km/h); 0 to 60 mph (100 km/h) 14.0 sec. Fuel consumption at constant 75 mph (120 km/h): 40.9 mpg.

Features: Equipment and fittings largely as for GT, but with new facia, and map light; illumination for ignition keyhole. Spoiler on rear. Alloy wheels optional.

DACIA (R)

Duster 4 × 4

Identity: The four-wheel drive Rumanian Dacia models are available in van and pick-up versions. All models are powered by 1400 cc engines and running gear is derived from Renault designs. Very economically priced.

Engine: Front-mounted, in-line four-cylinder with overhead valves. Bore 76 mm, stroke 77 mm; capacity 1397 cc. Power 65 bhp (48.4 kW) at 5250 rpm; torque 77.4 lb ft (10.5 Nm) at 3000 rpm. Compression 9.5-to-1.

Transmission: Four-wheel drive; four-speed manual gearbox; High and low ratio transfer box. Front freewheel hubs.

Suspension: Front, independent, wishbones, coil springs; telescopic dampers. Rear, live axle on semi-elliptic leaf springs; telescopic dampers.

Steering: Worm and roller. Power assistance: not available.

Brakes: Discs front, drums rear, servo-assisted.

Tyres: 175 × 14.   **Fuel tank:** 10.0 Imp. gall (45.5 litres).

Dimensions: Length 148.7 in (3777 mm), width 62.9 in (1600 mm), height 67.3 in (1740 mm), wheelbase 94.5 in (2400 mm).

Unladen weight: 2601.5 lb (1180 kg).

Performance: No data available at time of closing for press.

Features: Auto Dacia have been building cars in Rumania under licence from Renault for 20 years. The UK range includes utility pick-up and van, a GLX Estate and "leisure" version, the Roadster. There is also a rear wheel drive one-ton pick-up available.

DAIHATSU (J)   Charade diesel

Identity: New version of small Daihatsu launched Geneva 1983 with the world's first 1-litre diesel engine. Compact car but roomier than predecessor and with new body shape. Hatchback with two or four doors. Charade lettered above radiator grille identifies latest version.

Engine: Front-mounted transverse three-cylinder with ohc and balance shaft; diesel injection by Bosch; Daihatsu injector nozzles. Bore, 76 mm, stroke 73 mm; capacity 993 cc. Power 36 bhp (27 kW) at 4600 rpm; torque 43 lb ft (60 Nm) at 3500 rpm. Compression 21.5-to-1.

Transmission: Front-wheel drive; five-speed manual gearbox. Top gear speed at 1000 rpm: 21.0 mph (33.8 km/h).

Suspension: Front, independent, MacPherson struts; coil springs and telescopic dampers. Anti-roll bar. Rear, dead beam axle on trailing links with Panhard rod; coil springs and telescopic dampers. Anti-roll bar optional.

Steering: Rack and pinion. Power assistance: not available.

Brakes: Disc front, drums rear, servo-assisted.

Tyres: 145 SR 13.   **Fuel tank:** 7.5 Imp. gall (34 litres).

Dimensions: Length 139.8 in (3550 mm), width 61 in (1550 mm), height 54.9 in (1395 mm), wheelbase 91.3 in (2320 mm).

Unladen weight: 1532 lb (695 kg).

Performance (Works): Maximum speed 75 mph (121 km/h). Fuel consumption at constant 56 mph (90 km/h), 53.3 mpg.

Features: Phenomenally economical car, as I demonstrated in October 1983 with 90 mpg in an RAC-observed 200-mile economy drive. Very good low-speed pulling, and engine a lot more refined than one would expect from a three-cylinder diesel. Roomy and comfortable.

DAIHATSU (J)   Charmant 1600 LGX

Identity: New on British market in 1982, the Charmant is in marked contrast with the highly novel Charade, in being thoroughly conventional: three-box saloon body with four doors and engine in-line, driving rear wheels.

Engine: Front-mounted in-line four-cylinder with chain-driven single ohc. Alloy head on cast iron block. Breakerless ignition. Bore 85 mm, stroke 70 mm; capacity 1588 cc. Power 74 bhp (55 kW) at 5400 rpm; torque 87 lb ft (120 Nm) at 3600 rpm. Compression 9.0-to-1.

Transmission: Rear-wheel drive; five-speed manual gearbox; three-speed automatic optional. Final drive 3.91-to-1. Top gear speed at 1000 rpm: 19.3 mph (31.1 km/h).

Suspension: Front, independent, MacPherson struts; coil springs and telescopic dampers. Anti-roll bar. Rear, live axle on trailing links with Panhard rod. Coil springs and telescopic dampers.

Steering: Rack and pinion. Power assistance: not available.

Brakes: Discs front, drums rear, servo-assisted.

Tyres: 175/70 SR 13.   Fuel tank: 11 Imp. gall (50 litres).

Dimensions: Length 163.0 in (4150 mm), width 64 in (1625 mm), height 54.3 in (1379 mm), wheelbase 94.5 in (2400 mm).

Unladen weight: 2094 lb (950 kg).

Performance *Autocar* test: Maximum speed 94 mph (151 km/h). 0 to 60 mph (100 km/h) 13.2 sec. Fuel consumption at constant 75 mph (120 km/h), 31.1 mpg; overall test, 29.3 mpg.

Features: Quite pleasantly quiet and roomy car with good equipment for the price range. Disappointing features are the rather indifferent ride and low-geared steering.

DAIHATSU (J)   Domino

Identity: An example of Japan's prolific breed of 'minicars'. Introduced in UK late 1981, originally powered by a 547 cc engine. More at home as a town car than on motorways, when its lack of power is evident. Known as the Cuore outside the UK.

Engine: Front-mounted, transverse two-cylinder, water-cooled, with belt-driven ohc. Bore 76 mm, stroke 68 mm; capacity 617 cc. Power 30 bhp (22.4 kW) at 3000 rpm; torque 32 lb ft (43.4 Nm) at 3500 rpm. Compression 9.2-to-1.

Transmission: Front-wheel drive; four-speed manual gearbox. Top gear speed at 1000 rpm: 10.8 mph (17.5 km/h).

Suspension: Front, independent, MacPherson struts and coil springs; telescopic dampers. Rear, trailing arms and coil springs; telescopic dampers.

Steering: Rack and pinion. Power assistance: not available.

Brakes: Drums front and rear, no servo-assistance.

Tyres: 145 SR-10,   **Fuel tank:** 5.7 Imp. gall (26 litres).

Dimensions: Length 125.8 in (3195 mm), width 54.9 in (1394 mm), height 53.7 in (1364 mm), wheelbase 84.6 in (2149 mm).

Unladen weight: 1245 lb (2745 kg).

Performance *Autocar* test of 547 cc version: Maximum speed 72 mph (115.9 km/h); 0 to 60 mph (100 km/h) 26.6 sec. Fuel consumption at constant 56 mph (90 km/h): 50.4 mpg; overall test, 39.1 mpg.

Features: Fairly basic minicar with limited performance. Available only with three-door hatchback body. Very economically priced, and an acceptable runabout for shopping trips, with the advantage of easy parking—or take it into the store with you!

DAIMLER (GB)   Double-Six HE

Identity: Familiar lines of the Jaguar XJ lwb saloon with Daimler traditional fluted radiator grille and luxury fittings, and in the much more acceptable High Efficiency form with May combustion chambers, as introduced mid-1981. Changed in price and equipment October 1983.

Engine: Front-mounted V12-cylinder with single ohc each bank, Lucas injection and all-alloy construction. Bore 90 mm, stroke 70 mm; capacity 5345 cc. Power, 299 bhp (223 kW) at 5500 rpm; torque 318 lb ft (440 Nm) at 3000 rpm. Compression 12.5-to-1.

Transmission: Rear-wheel drive; GM Turbo Hydra-Matic 400 automatic transmission; no manual version. Top gear speed at 1000 rpm; 26.9 mph (43.3 km/h).

Suspension: Front, independent, wishbones and coil springs; anti-dive geometry; telescopic dampers. Anti-roll bar. Rear, independent, radius arms, transverse lower links, with twin coil springs and telescopic dampers each side.

Steering: Rack and pinion. Power assistance: standard.

Brakes: Discs front (vented) and rear, servo-assisted.

Tyres: 215/70 VR 15 Dunlop D7.   **Fuel tanks:** 20 Imp. gall total (91 litres).

Dimensions: Length 195 in (4951 mm), width 70 in (1770 mm), height 54 in (1374 mm), wheelbase 113 in (2865 mm).

Unladen weight: 4219 lb (1914 kg).

Performance *Autocar* test: Maximum speed, 150 mph (242 km/h). 0 to 60 mph (100 km/h) 8.1 sec. Fuel consumption, 21.5 mpg at constant 75 mph (120 km/h), overall test 16.4 mpg.

Features: Combination of comfort, speed, refinement, handling and quietness that few cars can match.

DODGE (USA)   600 Convertible

Identity: Mid-range model of the Dodge line-up is the 600. Available as a four-door sedan, two-door coupé or convertible, the engine options are: 2.2-litre fuel injection with or without turbocharger, or 2.6-litre carburettor unit.

Engine: Front-mounted four-cylinder with ohc; Bosch fuel injection and Garrett turbocharger. Bore, 87.4 mm, stroke 91.9 mm; capacity 2213 cc. Power 146 bhp (109 kW) at 5200 rpm; torque 168 lb ft (228 Nm) at 3600 rpm. Compression 8.1-to-1.

Transmission: Front-wheel drive; three-speed automatic Torqueflite. Top gear speed at 1000 rpm: 30.7 mph (49.4 km/h).

Suspension: Front, independent, MacPherson struts and coil springs; telescopic dampers. Anti-roll bar. Rear, dead beam axle on trailing arms with Panhard rod, coil springs; telescopic dampers.

Steering: Rack and pinion. Power assistance: optional.

Brakes: Discs front, drums rear, servo-assisted.

Tyres: P185/70 R14.   **Fuel tank:** 11.7 Imp. gall (53 litres).

Dimensions: Length 180.7 in (4590 mm), width 68.0 in (1727 mm), height 53.7 in (1364 mm), wheelbase 100.3 in (2548 mm).

Unladen weight: 2601 lb (1180 kg).

Performance (Works): Maximum speed 110 mph (180 km/h). Fuel consumption: 22 mpg (est.)

Features: Power-operated hood. The 600 ES Turbo is distinguishable by alloy wheels, discreet badging and louvres on bonnet for improved cooling. Electronic instruments and leather seats are standard.

DODGE (USA)   Shelby Charger

Identity: Claimed to have been America's first front-wheel drive sports coupé, the Dodge Charger has the option of 1.6-litre or 2.2-litre four-cylinder engines; the latter in turbocharged form becomes the Shelby Charger.

Engine: Front-mounted four-cylinder with ohc, Bosch fuel injection and Garrett AiResearch turbocharger. Bore 87.4 mm, stroke 91.9 mm; capacity 2213 cc. Power 146 bhp (109 kW) at 5200 rpm; torque 168 lb ft (228 Nm) at 3600 rpm. Compression 8.1-to-1.

Transmission: Front-wheel drive; five-speed manual gearbox with very high top gear. Top gear speed at 1000 rpm: 33.4 mph (53.8 km/h).

Suspension: Front, independent, MacPherson struts and coil springs; gas-filled telescopic dampers. Anti-roll bar. Rear, semi-independent, trailing arms, coil springs; telescopic dampers.

Steering: Rack and pinion. Power assistance: standard.

Brakes: Ventilated discs front, drums rear, servo-assisted.

Tyres: P205/50 VR 15.   **Fuel tank:** 10.8 Imp. gall (49 litres).

Dimensions: Length 174.8 in (4439 mm), width 66.1 in (1679 mm), height 50.7 in (1288 mm), wheelbase 96.5 in (2451 mm).

Unladen weight: 2215 lb (1004 kg).

Performance (est.): Maximum speed 120 mph (193 km/h); 0 to 60 mph (100 km/h) 8.0 sec. Fuel consumption: 23 mpg (est.).

Features: Addition of the turbocharger in the Shelby version is new for 1985. Distinctive sporting exterior. Low profile tyres. Sports bucket seats. Air conditioning available as an option.

Identity: The GTO is the fastest Ferrari road car ever. It's also exclusive, with only 200 built to qualify for Group B homologation in international racing regulations. Based on the 308, but with a longer wheelbase and powered by a twin turbocharged V8 engine. Latest version: Paris 1984. A thoroughbred supercar for the very wealthy.

Engine: Mid-mounted, longitudinal V8-cylinder with Weber-Marelli electronic injection and ignition and twin turbochargers, intercoolers and common wastegate. Bore 80.01 mm, stroke 70.99 mm; capacity 2855 cc. Power 400 bhp (298 kW) at 7000 rpm; torque 366 lb ft (496 Nm) at 3800 rpm. Compression 7.6-to-1.

Transmission: Rear-wheel drive; five-speed manual gearbox; with limited slip differential.

Suspension: Front, independent, wishbones, co-axial springs and telescopic dampers. Anti-roll bar. Rear, independent, wishbones, co-axial springs and telescopic dampers. Anti-roll bar.

Steering: Rack and pinion. Power assistance: not available.

Brakes: Ventilated discs front and rear, servo-assisted.

Tyres: F:225/50-16; R:265/50-16.   **Fuel tank:** 26.4 Imp. gall (120 litres).

Dimensions: Length 166.5 in (4230 mm), width 67.71 in (1720 mm), height 44.09 in (1120 mm), wheelbase 96.5 in (2451 mm).

Unladen weight: 2557 lb (1160 kg).

Performance (Works): Maximum speed 189 mph (304 km/h); 0 to 60 mph (100 km/h) 4.9 sec.

Features: The car's performance means Ferrari can once again claim the title 'world's fastest production car'. Wide use has been made of Ferrari's Formula 1 expertise in the design of special lightweight components.

FERRARI (I)   Testarossa

Identity: Newest model in the Ferrari stable is the exciting Testarossa, launched Paris 1984. With its Pininfarina-designed bodywork, this effectively replaces the BB512i, but the engine owes more to the 3-litre V12 currently used by Ferrari in Formula 1 racing.

Engine: Mid-mounted flat 12-cylinder with four valves per cylinder, twin camshafts per bank, Bosch fuel injection. Bore 82 mm, stroke 78 mm; capacity 4942 cc. Power 390 bhp (290 kW) at 6800 rpm; torque 361 lb ft (490 Nm) at 4500 rpm. Compression 9.2-to-1.

Transmission: Rear-wheel drive; five-speed manual gearbox; with limited slip differential. Top gear at 1000 rpm: 28.7 mph (46.2 km/h).

Suspension: Front, independent, double wishbones, helical springs; telescopic dampers. Anti-roll bar. Rear, independent, double wishbones, helical springs; telescopic dampers. Anti-roll bar.

Steering: Rack and pinion. Power assistance: not available.

Brakes: Ventilated discs front and rear, servo-assisted.

Tyres: F:225/50 VR-16; R:255/50 VR-16.   **Fuel tank:** 26.4 Imp. gall (120 litres).

Dimensions: Length 176.6 in (4485 mm), width 77.80 in (1976 mm), height 44.5 in (1130 mm), wheelbase 100.4 in (2550 mm).

Unladen weight: 3320 lb (1506 kg).

Performance (Works): Maximum speed 181 mph (291 km/h); 0 to 60 mph (100 km/h) 5.8 sec. Fuel consumption at constant 75 mph (120 km/h): 23.9 mpg.

Features: The Testarossa—Redhead—has many features gleaned from motor racing; the radiators are just ahead of the rear wheels. Bodywork is of aluminium alloy except for the doors and the cockpit which are steel. Inside seats are Connolly leather and air conditioning is standard.

Identity: Introduced 1983, the Bertone Cabrio conversion of the Strada—Ritmo in markets outside UK—is built by Bertone. Conversion has fixed roll-over bar but fully folding hood; two-door body. Birmingham 1984 saw introduction of the special Palinuro version with distinctive colour scheme; on market spring 1985.

Engine: Front-mounted transverse four-cylinder with alloy head and belt-driven ohc. Weber carb. Bore 86.4 mm, stroke 63.9 mm; capacity 1498 cc. Power 82 bhp (67 kW) at 5600 rpm; torque 88 lb ft (122 Nm) at 3000 rpm. Compression 9.2-to-1.

Transmission: Front-wheel drive; five-speed manual gearbox; no automatic option. Final drive 3.56-to-1. Top gear speed at 1000 rpm: 21.7 mph (34.9 km/h).

Suspension: Front, independent, MacPherson struts and coil springs; telescopic dampers. Anti-roll bar. Rear, independent, MacPherson struts and transverse leaf spring; telescopic dampers. Leaf spring provides anti-roll effect.

Steering: Rack and pinion. Power assistance: not available.

Brakes: Discs front, drums rear, servo-assisted.

Tyres: 165/65 SR 14.   **Fuel tank:** 12.1 Imp. gall (55 litres).

Dimensions: Length 158 in (4014 mm), width 65 in (1650 mm), height 55 in (1340 mm), wheelbase 96.4 in (2449 mm).

Unladen weight: 2051 lb (931 kg).

Performance (Works): Maximum speed 103 mph (166 km/h); 0 to 60 mph (100 km/h) 11.0 sec. Fuel consumption at constant 75 mph (120 km/h): 38.2 mpg.

Features: Inevitably there is some loss of structural strength as a result of the soft-top conversion, and some shake and rattles result, but the Cabrio provides pleasant fresh air motoring with the hood down.

Identity: The distinctive, chunky Panda became available with four-wheel-drive from September 1984, developed specially for the car by Steyr-Daimler-Puch. More powerful 965 cc Autobianchi engine. Special appeal as a low-cost go-anywhere vehicle promising low running costs.

Engine: Front-mounted transverse, four-cylinder with light alloy head and cast iron block. Twin choke Weber carb. Bore, 67.2 mm, stroke 68 mm; capacity 965 cc. Power 48 bhp (36 kW) at 5600 rpm; torque 51 lb ft (69 Nm) at 3500 rpm. Compression 9.2-to-1.

Transmission: Four-wheel drive; five-speed manual gearbox; four-wheel-drive selector lever. Top gear speed at 1,000 rpm: 15.8 mph (25.4 km/h).

Suspension: Front, independent, MacPherson struts, coil springs and telescopic dampers. Rear, live axle on leaf springs; telescopic dampers.

Steering: Rack and pinion. Power assistance: not available.

Brakes: Discs front, drums rear, servo-assisted.

Tyres: 145 SR-13.   **Fuel tank:** 7.7 Imp. gall (35 litres).

Dimensions: Length 133 in (3378 mm), width 58.5 in (1485 mm), height 57.5 in (1460 mm), wheelbase 85 in (2159 mm).

Unladen weight: 1678 lb (761 kg).

Performance (Works): Maximum speed 84 mph (135 km/h); 0 to 60 mph (100 km/h) 18.2 sec. Fuel consumption at constant 75 mph (120 km/h): 35.8 mpg.

Features: Visually it looks like a standard Panda; only the very subtle badging says four-wheel-drive. All the standard features of this cheeky little hatchback remain. Good carrying capacity, and now offered with added traction abilities in this additional version.

Identity: Promising new model launched September 1983 to replace Fiat's 131 Mirafiori range. Similar engines, but installed transversely and driving front wheels instead of rear. Choice of 1299, 1498 or 1585 cc petrol engines, or 1714 diesel. ES (energy saving) version has 1299 unit and special engine stop system to save fuel at traffic halts.

Engine: Front-mounted transverse, four-cylinder with ohc and alloy head (1600 has twin ohc). Toothed belt cam drive. Weber carb. Bore 86.4 mm, stroke 55.5 mm; capacity 1299 cc. Power 65 bhp (48 kW) at 5800 rpm; torque 72 lb ft (100 Nm) at 2900 rpm. Compression 9.6-to-1.

Transmission: Front-wheel drive; five-speed manual gearbox; automatic transmission option for 1498 model (Regata 85) only. Top gear speed at 1000 rpm: 21.0 mph (33.8 km/h).

Suspension: Front, independent, MacPherson struts; coil springs and telescopic dampers. Anti-roll bar. Rear, independent, MacPherson struts and lower wishbones; transverse leaf springs and telescopic dampers.

Steering: Rack and pinion; steering damper for Regata 85 and 100. Power assistance optional for 100 Super only.

Brakes: Discs front, drums rear, servo-assisted.

Tyres: 155 SR 13.   **Fuel tank**: 12.1 Imp. gall (55 litres).

Dimensions: Length 167.7 in (4260 mm), width 65 in (1650 mm), height 56 in (1420 mm), wheelbase 96.3 in (2448 mm).

Unladen weight: 1962 lb (890 kg).

Performance *Autocar* test: Maximum speed 97 mph (156 km/h); 0 to 60 mph (100 km/h) 13.2 sec. Fuel consumption at constant 75 mph (120 km/h): 40.4 mpg; overall test 35.5 mpg.

Features: Very roomy car, easy to drive, and offering good comfort and reasonably low noise level.

FIAT (I)   Regata 100S

Identity: Top version of the Fiat Regata range, which replaced the former Mirafiori models, is the 100 Super, with twin ohc engine. Same four-door saloon body as for the ES, but without the window deflectors. Divided rear seat optional, folds for extra luggage space.

Engine: Front-mounted transverse four-cylinder with belt-driven twin ohc. Marelli Digiplex ignition. Weber twin-choke carb. Bore 84 mm; stroke 71.5 mm; capacity 1585 cc. Power 100 bhp (73.5 kW) at 5900 rpm; torque 96 lb ft (133 Nm) at 3800 rpm. Comp. 9.3-to-1.

Transmission: Front-wheel drive; five-speed manual gearbox; no automatic transmission availability for 100 (85 Super option only).

Suspension: Front, independent, wishbones and coil springs; telescopic dampers. Anti-roll bar. Rear, independent wishbones and transverse leaf spring; telescopic dampers. Leaf spring provides anti-roll effect.

Steering: Rack and pinion with vibration damper. Power assistance: optional.

Brakes: Discs front, drums rear, servo-assisted.

Tyres: 165/65 SR 14.   **Fuel tank:** 12.1 Imp. gall (55 litres).

Dimensions: Length 167.7 in (4260 mm), width 65 in (1650 mm), height 55.6 in (1412 mm), wheelbase 96.3 in (2448 mm).

Unladen weight: 2138 lb (970 kg).

Performance *Autocar* test: Maximum speed 108 mph (174 km/h); 0 to 60 mph (100 km/h) 9.9 sec. Fuel consumption at constant 75 mph (120 km/h): 35.8 mpg; overall test, 29.1 mpg.

Features: Well-equipped car offering promising combination of performance and economy. Super versions come with electric window lifts, central locking, check control system, rev counter, halogen headlamps, electrically-operated heating and ventilation controls, and economy indicator.

Identity: Quickest version of the Strada range, with impressive performance suited to the famous Italian Abarth name. Highly tuned version of the 2-litre twin ohc engine. Uprated suspension contributes to excellent handling characteristics.

Engine: Front-mounted transverse, four-cylinder with aluminium head and cast iron block. Bore 84 mm, stroke 90 mm; capacity 1995 cc. Power 130 bhp (95.6 kW) at 5900 rpm; torque 130 lb ft (176 Nm) at 3600 rpm. Compression 9.45-to-1.

Transmission: Front-wheel drive; five-speed manual gearbox. Top gear speed at 1000 rpm: 19.8 mph (31.9 km/h).

Suspension: Front, independent, MacPherson struts and coil springs; telescopic dampers. Anti-roll bar. Rear, independent, struts, single transverse leaf spring; telescopic dampers.

Steering: Rack and pinion. Power assistance: not available.

Brakes: Discs front, drums rear, servo-assisted.

Tyres: 185/60 HR-14.   **Fuel tank:** 12.1 Imp. gall (55 litres).

Dimensions: Length 158 in (4013 mm), width 65.5 in (1663 mm), height 54.7 in (1389 mm), wheelbase 96.2 in (2443 mm).

Unladen weight: 2168 lb (983 kg).

Performance *Autocar* test: Maximum speed 118 mph (190 km/h); 0 to 60 mph (100 km/h) 8.2 sec. Fuel consumption at constant 75 mph (120 km/h): 32.1 mpg; overall test, 26.3 mpg.

Features: One of the newest of the 'hot hatchback' brigade. Performance and handling are improved, together with suitable packaging of spoilers, wheel arch extensions, rally-type bucket seats and low-profile tyres.

Identity: Replacement for Fiat's long-serving 127 model, the Uno was launched early 1983; on British market June. Hatchback with rounded front and Fiat family grille with diagonal bars; choice of two or four side doors, and three engine options—45, 55 and 70—plus ES (energy saving) version of 45 model.

Engine: Front-mounted transverse four-cylinder with gearbox in line. Belt-driven single ohc. Weber carb. Alloy head. Bore 86.4 mm, stroke 55.5 mm; capacity 1301 cc. Power 70 bhp (52 kW) at 5700 rpm; torque 74 lb ft (102 Nm) at 2900 rpm. Compression 9.1-to-1.

Transmission: Front-wheel drive; five-speed manual gearbox; no automatic transmission available. Uno 45 has four-speed gearbox. Top gear speed at 1000 rpm: 21.3 mph (34.3 km/h).

Suspension: Front, independent, MacPherson struts; coil springs and telescopic dampers. Anti-roll bar. Rear, semi-independent, torsion beam axle and trailing arms; coil springs and telescopic dampers.

Steering: Rack and pinion. Power assistance: not available.

Brakes: Discs front, drums rear, servo-assisted.

Tyres: 155/70 SR 13.   **Fuel tank:** 9.2 Imp. gall (42 litres).

Dimensions: Length 143.5 in (3644 mm), width 60.9 in (1548 mm), height 56.4 in (1432 mm), wheelbase 93 in (2362 mm).

Unladen weight: 1653 lb (750 kg).

Performance *Autocar* test: Maximum speed 102 mph (164 km/h); 0 to 60 mph (100 km/h) 12.1 sec. Fuel consumption at constant 75 mph (120 km/h): 43.5 mpg; overall test, 35.3 mpg.

Features: Lively little hatchback with functional appearance (though rather short in the tail), and quite good accommodation for a small car. Easy to drive; good heating and ventilation. Super models have halogen headlamps, lockable fuel cap, clock, trip recorder, and tinted glass.

Identity: Delightful mid-engined two-seater with removable Targa panel; car offers safe, fun motoring with exceptionally good roadholding. Poor engine access one of the few drawbacks. Larger engine version with five-speed gearbox introduced Birmingham 1982. Bodywork by Bertone.

Engine: Mid-mounted four-cylinder with belt-driven ohc, and Weber twin-choke carb. Bore 86.4 mm, stroke 63.9 mm; capacity 1498 cc. Power 85 bhp (63 kW) at 6000 rpm; torque 87 lb ft (120 Nm) at 3200 rpm. Compression 9.2-to-1.

Transmission: Rear-wheel drive; five-speed manual gearbox; (no automatic transmission version available). All gears indirect, fifth geared-up. Top gear speed at 1000 rpm: 18.3 mph (29.5 km/h).

Suspension: Front, independent, MacPherson struts, coil springs and telescopic dampers. Rear, independent, MacPherson struts, coil springs and telescopic dampers. No anti-roll bar front or rear—yet little roll.

Steering: Rack and pinion. Power assistance: not available.

Brakes: Discs front and rear, no servo.

Tyres: 165/70 SR 13.   **Fuel tank:** 10.6 Imp. gall (48 litres).

Dimensions: Length 156 in (1970 mm), width 62 in (1570 mm), height 46.5 in (1180 mm), wheelbase 86.8 in (2204 mm).

Unladen weight: 2010 lb (912 kg).

Performance *Autocar* test: Maximum speed 106 mph (171 km/h); 0 to 60 mph (100 km/h) 11.0 sec. Fuel consumption, 36.8 mpg (at constant 75 mph) (120km/h) overall test, 26.1 mpg.

Features: Stereo radio and alloy wheels standard. Small luggage space front and rear, and detachable roof panel restows at front. Pop-up headlamps. Automatic choke.

Identity: Joining the sudden spurt of interest in convertible bodywork was the very neatly executed Escort Cabriolet from Ford, launched Frankfurt, 1983. It is based on the Escort GL, and has fixed roll bar behind the front seat but is otherwise fully open when the top is down. Three versions are offered: 1.3, 1.6, and 1.6 with the fuel injection engine as fitted in the XR3i (details follow).

Engine: Front-mounted transverse four-cylinder with alloy head, belt driven ohc, and inclined valves worked by hydraulic tappets. Bosch K-Jetronic injection. Bore 80 mm, stroke 79.5 mm; capacity 1598 cc. Power 103 bhp (77 kW) at 6000 rpm; torque 100 lb ft (138 Nm) at 4800 rpm. Compression 9.5-to-1.

Transmission: Front-wheel drive; five-speed manual gearbox; 1.3 model has four-speed, with five-speed optional. No automatic option. Top gear speed at 1000 rpm: 19.5 mph (31.4 km/h).

Suspension: Front, independent, MacPherson struts; coil springs and Bilstein gas telescopic dampers. Anti-roll bar. Rear, independent, MacPherson struts; varying rate coil springs and Bilstein dampers.

Steering: Rack and pinion. Power assistance: not available.

Brakes: Vented discs front, drums rear, servo-assisted.

Tyres: 185/60 HR 14.   **Fuel tank:** 8.8 Imp. gall (40 litres).

Dimensions: Length 160 in (4059 mm), width 62.5 in (1588 mm), height 52.6 in (1336 mm), wheelbase 94.5 in (2398 mm).

Unladen weight: 2040 lb (925 kg).

Performance *Autocar* test (XR3i): Maximum speed 116 mph (187 km/h); 0 to 60 mph (100 km/h) 8.6 sec. Fuel consumption at constant 75 mph (120 km/h): 37.2 mpg; overall test, 30.5 mpg.

Features: Hood folds neatly down with scissors action of frame, and is held by two catches; it can then be protected with a PVC tonneau cover.

FORD (GB, D)   Escort RS Turbo

Identity: Announced at Paris 1984, this is the most powerful version of Ford's best-selling Escort. First volume-produced turbocharged passenger car to have a limited-slip differential as standard equipment.

Engine: Front-mounted transverse four-cylinder with aluminium head and cast iron block. OHC with hydraulic tappets and Garrett AiResearch turbocharger. Bore 80 mm, stroke 79.5 mm; capacity 1598 cc. Power 132 bhp (97 kW) at 6000 rpm; torque 132.6 lb ft (180 Nm) at 3000 rpm. Compression 8.3-to-1.

Transmission: Front-wheel drive; five-speed manual gearbox with limited-slip differential as standard. Top gear speed at 1000 rpm: 20.3 mph (32.7 km/h).

Suspension: Front, independent, MacPherson struts, coil springs lateral and longitudinal lower links; telescopic dampers. Anti-roll bar. Rear, MacPherson struts, coil springs, lateral and longitudinal lower links; telescopic dampers. Anti-roll bar.

Steering: Rack and pinion. Power assistance: not available.

Brakes: Ventilated discs front, drums rear, servo-assisted.

Tyres: 195/50 VR 15.   **Fuel tank:** 8.8 Imp. gall (40 litres).

Dimensions: Length 159.8 in (4059 mm), width 62.5 in (1587 mm), height 52.6 in (1336 mm), wheelbase 94.1 in (2390 mm).

Performance (est.): Maximum speed 125 mph (206 km/h); 0 to 60 mph (100 km/h) 8.2 sec. Fuel consumption: 28 mpg (est.).

Features: Developed from the very successful XR3i, the RS Turbo has been built to compete in national and international motorsport events in both Group N and Group A categories. Available only with three-door body, featuring comprehensive aerodynamic aids, racing seats and low-profile tyres.

FORD (USA)

EXP Turbo

Identity: Using many of the components of the American Escort, the EXP is Ford's sporting 2 + 2. Powered by the 1.6-litre engine of the Escort, it comes in carburettor form or with fuel injection, and turbocharged. Trim levels are standard, luxury coupé or Turbo Coupé.

Engine: Front-mounted transverse four-cylinder with electron fuel injection and single turbocharger. Bore 80 mm, stroke 79.52 mm; capacity 1599 cc. Power 120 bhp (89 kW) at 5200 rpm; torque 120 lb ft (163 Nm) at 3400 rpm. Compression 8.0-to-1.

Transmission: Front-wheel drive; five-speed manual gearbox. Top gear speed at 1000 rpm: 24.2 mph (39 km/h).

Suspension: Front, independent, MacPherson struts and coil springs; telescopic dampers. Anti-roll bar. Rear, independent, trailing arms, coil springs; telescopic dampers.

Steering: Rack and pinion. Power assistance: optional.

Brakes: Ventilated discs front, drums rear, servo-assisted.

Tyres: P165/80 R-13.   **Fuel tank** 10.7 Imp. gall (49 litres).

Dimensions: Length 170.3 in (4325 mm), width 65.9 in (1675 mm), height 50.6 in (1285 mm), wheelbase 94.3 in (2395 mm).

Unladen weight: 2204 lb (1000 kg).

Performance (est.): Maximum speed 98 mph (158 km/h). Fuel consumption: 28 mpg (est.).

Features: The Turbo Coupé version has front air dam, rear spoiler and low profile tyres on aluminium alloy wheels. The sporty character continues inside with bucket seats. New for 1985 is the stereo radio cassette player.

FORD (GB, D, B, E)   Fiesta Ghia 1.1

Identity: New lease of life for Fiesta range came in August 1983, when front panelwork was reshaped for improved aerodynamics and engine choice was extended. Fiesta also available—from 1984—as diesel version with same unit as Orion diesel (p. 78) with Popular Plus or L trim. Five-speed gearbox optional, and choice of Popular Plus, L and Ghia trim for 1.1. Two-door hatchback body.

Engine: Front-mounted transverse four-cylinder with cast iron head and block; pushrod ohv. 1300 and 1600 have alloy head and ohc. Bore 74 mm, stroke 65 mm; capacity 1117 cc. Power 50 bhp (37 kW) at 6000 rpm; torque 72 lb ft (100 Nm) at 2700 rpm. Comp. 9.5-to-1.

Transmission: Front-wheel drive; four-speed manual gearbox; Five-speed optional (standard on 1300 and 1600). No automatic option. Top gear speed at 1000 rpm: 21.3 mph (34.3 km/h).

Suspension: Front, independent, MacPherson struts and coil springs; telescopic dampers. Anti-roll bar triangulated to lower links. Rear, dead beam axle with trailing arms and Panhard rod. Coil springs and telescopic dampers. Anti-roll bar with Sport pack.

Steering: Rack and pinion. Power assistance: not available.

Brakes: Discs front, drums rear, servo-assisted.

Tyres: 135 SR 13.   **Fuel tank:** 7.5 Imp. gall (34 litres).

Dimensions: Length 143.6 in (3648 mm), width 61 in (1549 mm), height 52.2 in (1327 mm), wheelbase 90 in (2288 mm).

Unladen weight: 1664 lb (755 kg).

Performance *Autocar* test: Maximum speed 86 mph (138 km/h); 0 to 60 mph (100 km/h) 16.8 sec. Fuel consumption (five-speed) at constant 75 mph (120 km/h): 41.5 mpg; overall test, 37.2 mpg.

Features: Pleasing small car with generous equipment and high standard of trim and finish in this luxury Ghia form.

FORD (USA)   Mustang Convertible

Identity: America's sporting four-seater convertible goes on for 1985 with few changes, but slightly revised grille with open slot instead of former horizontal slats identifies 1985 model. Base model has 2.3-litre four-cylinder engine; others are a performance version from Ford's Special Vehicle Operations (SVO), and the V8 GT (details below).

Engine: Front-mounted longitudinal V8-cylinder with pushrod ohc. Holley four-choke carb. Bore 101.6 mm, stroke 76.2 mm; capacity 4942 cc. Power 174 bhp (130 kW) at 4000 rpm; torque 240 lb ft (332 Nm) at 2400 rpm. Compression 8.3-to-1.

Transmission: Rear-wheel drive; five-speed manual gearbox; three-speed automatic optional, with overdrive. Top gear speed at 1000 rpm: 32 mph (51.5 km/h).

Suspension: Front, independent, MacPherson struts and coil springs; telescopic dampers. Anti-roll bar. Rear, live-axle on four links, with coil springs; telescopic dampers.

Steering: Rack and pinion. Power assistance: optional.

Brakes: Discs front, drums rear, servo-assisted.

Tyres: P185/75 R14.   **Fuel tank:** 12.8 Imp. gall (58 litres).

Dimensions: Length 179.1 in (4549 mm), width 69.1 in (1755 mm), height 51.9 in (1318 mm), wheelbase 100.5 in (2553 mm).

Unladen weight: 3020 lb (1370 kg).

Performance (Works): Maximum speed 122 mph (197 km/h).

Features: Choice of bodywork is coupé, hatchback or convertible. Integral fog lamps identify the GT model, which has sports seats and new cloth trim. Detail improvements for 1985 include better engine efficiency.

FORD (GB, D) Orion 1.6 Diesel

Identity: First application of the new Ford 1.6 diesel engine was in the Orion saloon derivative of the Escort, but it quickly followed in other models including the Escort and Fiesta. Exceptional economy; five-speed gearbox standard.

Engine: Front-mounted transverse in-line four-cylinder with cast iron head and block; single ohc belt-driven from gear-driven injection pump. Bore 80 mm, stroke 79.5 mm; capacity 1598 cc. Power 54 bhp (40 kW) at 4800 rpm; torque 69 lb ft (95 Nm) at 3000 rpm. Compression 21.5-to-1.

Transmission: Front-wheel drive; five-speed manual gearbox; no automatic option for diesel. Top gear speed at 1000 rpm: 19.6 mph (31.5 km/h).

Suspension: Front, independent, MacPherson struts; coil springs and telescopic dampers. Anti-roll bar. Rear, independent, MacPherson struts; coil springs and rising rate telescopic gas-filled dampers.

Steering: Rack and pinion. Power assistance: not available.

Brakes: Discs front, drums rear, servo-assisted.

Tyres: 155 SR 13.   **Fuel tank:** 10.5 Imp. gall (47.7 litres).

Dimensions: Length 156 in (3970 mm), width 64.5 in (1640 mm), height 54.3 in (1380 mm), wheelbase 94.3 in (2395 mm).

Unladen weight: 2094 lb (950 kg).

Performance (Works): Maximum speed 91 mph (147 km/h); 0 to 60 mph (100 km/h) 18.1 sec. Fuel consumption at constant 75 mph (120 km/h): 48.7 mpg.

Features: Prime purchase for an efficient, compact car for business use giving impressively low running costs. A very acceptable diesel, giving quite lively performance and very easy to drive.

FORD (GB, D)   Sierra 1.8 automatic

Identity: Ford's Sierra was given subtle styling changes for 1985, and the four-lamp Ghia front-end was adopted for L and GL petrol versions as well. The most important changes are under the skin, with a new engine of 1.8-litre capacity, and a new four-speed automatic gearbox.

Engine: Front-mounted in-line four-cylinder with electronic ignition and two-venturi carburettor. Bore, 86.2 mm, stroke 77 mm; capacity 1796 cc. Power 90 bhp (66 kW) at 5300 rpm; torque 101.7 lb ft (138 Nm) at 3300 rpm. Compression 9.5-to-1.

Transmission: Rear-wheel drive; five-speed manual or four-speed automatic with lock-up overdrive. Top gear speed at 1000 rpm: 25.0 mph (40.2 km/h).

Suspension: Front, independent, MacPherson struts, coil springs plus polyurethane auxiliary springs and bump stops. Rear, independent, semi-trailing arms, coil springs plus polyurethane auxiliary springs and bump stops, telescopic dampers.

Steering: Rack and pinion. Power assistance: optional.

Brakes: Discs front, drums rear, servo-assisted.

Tyres: 195/70 HR 13.   **Fuel tank:** 13.2 Imp. gall (60 litres).

Dimensions: Length 176.8 in (4490 mm), width 67.7 in (1720 mm), height 54.8 in (1392 mm), wheelbase 102.7 in (2609 mm).

Unladen weight: 2280 lb (1035 kg).

Performance *Autocar* test for 2-litre, manual version: Maximum speed 111 mph (178 km/h); 0 to 60 mph (100 km/h) 10.1 sec. Fuel consumption at constant 75 mph (120 km/h): 36.7 mpg; overall test, 27.5 mpg.

Features: A comfortable and well-balanced car, capable of taking large loads in its stride.

FORD (GB, D)   Sierra 2.0 GL Estate Car

Identity: After the 1982 launch of Ford's Sierra replacement for the Cortina, it took a little while for production of the Estate car models to start up. They began to appear in Britain early in 1983.

Engine: Front-mounted longitudinal four-cylinder with belt-driven single ohc and fingers for valve operation. Weber twin-choke carb. Bore 90.8 mm, stroke 77 mm; capacity 1993 cc. Power 103 bhp (77 kW) at 5200 rpm; torque 113 lb ft (157 Nm) at 4000 rpm. Compression 9.2-to-1.

Transmission: Rear-wheel drive; five-speed manual gearbox; four-speed automatic transmission optional. Top gear speed at 1000 rpm: 24.8 mph (40.0 km/h).

Suspension: Front, independent, MacPherson struts; coil springs and polyurethane auxiliary springs and bump stops. Telescopic dampers. Anti-roll bar. Rear, independent, semi-trailing arms; coil springs and polyurethane auxiliary springs and bump stops; telescopic dampers.

Steering: Rack and pinion. Power assistance: optional.

Brakes: Discs front, drums rear, servo-assisted.

Tyres: 195/70 HR 13.   **Fuel tank:** 13.2 Imp. gall (60 litres).

Dimensions: Length 176.8 in (4490 mm), width 67.7 in (1720 mm), height 54.8 in (1392 mm), wheelbase 102.7 in (2609 mm).

Unladen weight: 2346 lb (1064 kg).

Performance *Autocar* test: Maximum speed 111 mph (179 km/h); 0 to 60 mph (100 km/h) 10.1 sec. Fuel consumption at constant 75 mph (120 km/h): 36.7 mpg; overall test, 27.5 mpg.

Features: Comfortable car with very good ride and well-balanced handling. Suspension takes heavy load very well, and curved rear door enables door to close when fully packed at rear. Back seat folds.

FORD (USA)   Thunderbird Turbo Coupé

Identity: Detail changes are made to the Thunderbird for 1985—mainly improved and slightly crisper appearance, and the engine in the Turbo Coupé gives a little more power than before. There are also Elan and FILA models.

Engine: Front-mounted longitudinal four-cylinder with belt-driven ohc. Hydraulic tappets. Electronic injection and Garrett turbocharger. Bore 96.0 mm, stroke 79.4 mm; capacity 2301 cc. Power 150 bhp (112 kW) at 4600 rpm; torque 178 lb ft (246 Nm) at 3600 rpm. Compression 9.0-to-1.

Transmission: Rear-wheel drive; five-speed manual gearbox; three-speed automatic transmission optional. Top gear speed at 1000 rpm: 25 mph (40.2 km/h).

Suspension: Front, independent, MacPherson struts with coil springs bearing on to lower arms; telescopic dampers. Anti-roll bar. Rear, live axle on four-locating links and coil springs; telescopic dampers, plus horizontal gas filled dampers for cornering loads. Anti-roll bar.

Steering: Varying ratio rack and pinion. Power assistance: standard.

Brakes: Discs front, drums rear, servo-assisted.

Tyres: P195/75 R 14.   **Fuel tank:** 17.5 Imp. gall (80 litres).

Dimensions: Length 197.6 in (5019 mm), width 71.1 in (1806 mm), height 53.2 in (1351 mm), wheelbase 104 in (2641 mm).

Unladen weight: 3037 lb (1378 kg).

Performance (Works): Maximum speed 110 mph (177 km/h). Fuel consumption overall (test), 24 mpg.

Features: Electronic instrumentation with graphic readouts in new instrument panel are significant new features for 1985. New split-bench reclining seat in cloth trim. Gear ratios and gear change action improved.

FORD (GB, D)   Tickford Capri

Identity: New at Birmingham 1982, the exciting high performance version of the Ford Capri 2.8i by Aston Martin Tickford went into small-scale production with full Type Approval October 1983. Big air dam with brake cooling inlets at front; rear spoiler and side fairings. Turbocharged engine and very high performance.

Engine: Front-mounted V6-cylinder with IHI turbocharger. Bosch K-Jetronic injection. Bore 93 mm, stroke 68.5 mm; capacity 2792 cc. Power 205 bhp (153 kW) at 5000 rpm; torque 260 lb ft (353 Nm) at 3500 rpm. Compression 9.2-to-1.

Transmission: Rear-wheel drive; five-speed manual gearbox; ZF limited slip diff. Final drive 3.09-to-1. Top gear speed at 1000 rpm: 25.8 mph (41.5 km/h).

Suspension: Front, independent, MacPherson struts and transverse links; coil springs and Bilstein telescopic dampers. Anti-roll bar. Rear, live axle on semi-elliptic leaf springs, with additional 'A' locating links. Bilstein gas filled telescopic dampers.

Steering: Rack and pinion. Power assistance: not available.

Brakes: Vented discs front, solid discs rear, servo-assisted.

Tyres: 205/60 VR 13.   **Fuel tank:** 12.8 Imp. gall (58 litres).

Dimensions: Length 171.4 in (4352 mm), width 67 in (1702 mm), height 51 in (1295 mm), wheelbase 101 in (2565 mm).

Unladen weight: 2690 lb (1220 kg).

Performance (Works): Maximum speed 140 mph (224 km/h); 0 to 60 mph (100 km/h) 6.0 sec. Fuel consumption at constant 75 mph (120 km/h): 27.4 mpg.

Features: Recaro seats trimmed in velour, with leather as option. Tilting/sliding sunroof. Very competently executed conversion.

FORD (GB, D, B, E)   Fiesta XR2

Identity: Ford's successful Fiesta range is topped by the XR2. In latest form, revised 1984, it has the CVH overhead camshaft engine, with carburettor, and gains the valuable addition of a fifth gear to the previous four-speed gearbox, giving much quieter cruising.

Engine: Front-mounted transverse four-cylinder with Weber down-draught twin-choke carburettor. Bore 79.96 mm, stroke 79.52 mm; capacity 1597 cc. Power 96 bhp (71 kW) at 6000 rpm; torque 98 lb ft (133 Nm) at 4000 rpm. Compression 9.5-to-1.

Transmission: Front-wheel drive; five-speed manual gearbox. Top gear speed at 1000 rpm: 23 mph (37 km/h).

Suspension: Front, independent, MacPherson struts and coil springs; telescopic dampers. Rear, dead beam axle, on four links and Panhard rod, coil springs; telescopic dampers. Anti-roll bar.

Steering: Rack and pinion. Power assistance: not available.

Brakes: Ventilated discs front, drums rear, servo-assisted.

Tyres: 185/60 HR-13.   **Fuel tank:** 8.8 Imp. gall (40 litres).

Dimensions: Length 146 in (3710 mm), width 63.8 in (1620 mm), height 52.6 in (1335 mm), wheelbase 90.2 in (2290 mm).

Unladen weight: 1851 lb (840 kg).

Performance *Autocar* test: Maximum speed 107 mph (172 km/h); 0 to 60 mph (100 km/h) 10.2 sec. Fuel consumption at constant 75 mph (120 km/h): 37.7 mpg; overall test, 29.9 mpg.

Features: A refined and easy-to-drive hot hatch with exciting performance together with the advantages of the hatchback, split rear seat and large load area. A practical fun car.

Identity: After many years of building cars under licence for Fiat, the five-door Polonez was the first car to be built to FSO's own design. Mechanically, however, much is based on the Fiat 125. Launched as the 1500 in 1968, it became the LE for 1984.

Engine: Front-mounted in-line four-cylinder with pushrod ohv. Alloy head. Weber twin-choke carb. Bore 77 mm, stroke 79.5 mm; capacity 1481 cc. Power 82 bhp (61 kW) at 5250 rpm; torque 84 lb ft (116 Nm) at 3400 rpm. Compression 9.2-to-1.

Transmission: Rear-wheel drive; five-speed manual gearbox. Top gear speed at 1000 rpm: 18.4 mph (29.6 km/h).

Suspension: Front, independent, wishbones and coil springs; telescopic dampers. Anti-roll bar. Rear, live rear axle on semi-elliptic leaf springs; telescopic dampers.

Steering: Worm and roller. Power assistance: not available.

Brakes: Discs front, drums rear, servo-assisted.

Tyres: 175 SR-13.   **Fuel tank:** 10 Imp. gall (45 litres).

Dimensions: Length 168 in (4272 mm), width 65 in (1650 mm), height 54.3 in (1380 mm), wheelbase 99 in (2509 mm).

Unladen weight: 2513 lb (1140 kg).

Performance *Autocar* test: Maximum speed 93 mph (158 km/h); 0 to 60 mph (100 km/h) 16.0 sec. Fuel consumption at constant 75 mph (120 km/h): 30.7 mpg; overall test, 21.4 mpg.

Features: By today's standards, the Polonez shows its age. Ponderous handling and an indifferent ride. Interior fittings, too, are crude and old-fashioned. Appeal remains the carrying capacity in relation to low price.

GINETTA (GB)

Identity: One of the few remaining 'build it yourself' sports cars. The Ginetta G4 is supplied in component form for home assembly. Tubular steel chassis, Ford engine and glass fibre bodywork. Two-seater; Ford engine.

Engine: Front-mounted four-cylinder with pushrod ohv; Weber carburettor. Bore 81 mm, stroke 77.6 mm; capacity 1599 cc. Power 88 bhp (66 kW) at 5500 rpm; torque 92 lb ft (127 Nm) at 3500 rpm. Compression 9.2-to-1.

Transmission: Rear-wheel drive; four-speed manual gearbox; close ratios. Top gear speed at 1000 rpm: 18.1 mph (29.1 km/h).

Suspension: Front, independent, wishbones and coil springs; telescopic dampers. Rear, live axle on trailing arms, radius rods and Panhard rod. Coil springs and telescopic dampers.

Steering: Rack and pinion. Power assistance: not available.

Brakes: Discs front, drums rear, servo-assisted.

Tyres: 165/SR 13.   **Fuel tank:** 9.9 Imp. gall (45 litres).

Dimensions: Length 147 in (3733 mm), width 62 in (1575 mm), height 42 in (1067 mm), wheelbase 84 in (2134 mm).

Unladen weight: 1230 lb (558 kg).

Performance *Autocar* test: Maximum speed 113 mph (182 km/h); 0 to 60 mph (100 km/h) 7.6 sec. Fuel consumption overall test, 27.5 mpg.

Features: A performance sports car for the enthusiast. Poor weather protection, and folding hood is difficult to erect; but fun to drive. Restricted luggage space, since the boot is largely filled by the spare wheel. Unusually, the fuel filler cap is also in the boot.

HONDA (J)   Accord

Identity: Often described as the most 'European' of the Japanese manufacturers, Honda introduced the revised Accord at the 1983 Frankfurt show. Available as a two-door plus hatch or a four-door saloon with either 1.6- or 1.8-litre engine.

Engine: Front-mounted in-line four-cylinder with two inlet and one exhaust valves per cylinder. Bore 80 mm, stroke 91 mm; capacity 1829 cc. Power 100 bhp (74.5 kW) at 5800 rpm; torque 109 lb ft (150 Nm) at 3500 rpm. Compression 9.1-to-1.

Transmission: Front-wheel drive; five-speed manual gearbox; four-speed automatic transmission optional. Top gear speed at 1000 rpm: 22.0 mph (35.4 km/h).

Suspension: Front, independent, MacPherson struts, coil springs; telescopic dampers. Rear, independent, MacPherson struts, coil springs; telescopic dampers. Anti-roll bar.

Steering: Rack and pinion. Power assistance: standard.

Brakes: Ventilated discs front, drums rear, servo-assisted.

Tyres: 165 SR-13.   **Fuel tank:** 13.2 Imp. gall (60 litres).

Dimensions: (Hatchback) Length 167.5 in (4255 mm), width 65.5 in (1665 mm), height 53.3 in (1355 mm), wheelbase 96.5 in (2450 mm).

Unladen weight: 2182.5 lb (990 kg).

Performance *Autocar* test: Maximum speed 95 mph (153 km/h); 0 to 60 mph (100 km/h) 12.1 sec. Fuel consumption at constant 75 mph (120 km/h): 34.4 mpg; overall test, 31.7 mpg.

Features: Sound design, well trimmed and finished. Car drives, rides and performs very well. High level of specification in Executive trim, with air conditioning available on the saloon version.

HONDA (J)   Jazz

Identity: Called the City when introduced at the Tokyo Show in 1982, this tall and high supermini is the Jazz in the UK. Unusual styling with high roof, steeply raked windscreen and abbreviated tail. The mechanical side is quite conventional, with transverse engine and front drive.

Engine: Front-mounted transverse four-cylinder with aluminium alloy head and block. Bore 66 mm, stroke 90 mm; capacity 1231 cc. Power 56 bhp (41 kW) at 5000 rpm; torque 69 lb ft (51 Nm) at 3500 rpm. Compression 10.2-to-1.

Transmission: Front-wheel drive; five-speed manual gearbox. Top gear speed at 1000 rpm; 22.0 mph (35.5 km/h).

Suspension: Front, independent, MacPherson struts and coil springs; telescopic dampers. Anti-roll bar. Rear, independent, lower wishbones and coil springs; telescopic dampers. Anti-roll bar.

Steering: Rack and pinion. Power assistance: not available.

Brakes: Discs front, drums rear, servo-assisted.

Tyres: 145SR-14.   **Fuel tank:** 9.0 Imp. gall (41 litres).

Dimensions: Length 133 in (3381 mm), width 61.8 in (1570 mm), height 57.9 in (1470 mm), wheelbase 87.4 in (2220 mm).

Unladen weight: 1556 lb (706 kg).

Performance *Autocar* test: Maximum speed 88 mph (142 km/h); 0 to 60 mph (100 km/h) 13.4 sec. Fuel consumption at constant 75 mph (120 km/h): 40.9 mpg; overall test, 35.3 mpg.

Features: The rather box-like shape gives the Honda Jazz a poor drag coefficient and a correspondingly low top speed. Yet its low weight does allow sprightly performance, and in spite of the short wheelbase, the ride is quite good. Removable smoked glass sun panel standard.

HYUNDAI (K)   Stellar

Identity: Launched Motorfair, 1983, the Korean-built Stellar is a four-door saloon with Italian styling and tidy, swept-back front with oblong headlamps. Mitsubishi-licensed engine and transmission, and conventional layout.

Engine: Front-mounted longitudinal four-cylinder with alloy head and single ohc. Bore 76.9 mm, stroke 86 mm; capacity 1597 cc. Power 98.6 bhp (74 kW) at 6300 rpm; torque 83 lb ft (115 Nm) at 4000 rpm. Compression 8.5-to-1.

Transmission: Rear-wheel drive; four-speed manual gearbox; Stellar SL and GSL have five-speed; three-speed automatic optional. Top gear speed at 1000 rpm: 18.4 mph (29.6 km/h).

Suspension: Front, independent, wishbones and coil springs; telescopic dampers. Anti-roll bar. Rear, live axle on four trailing progressive rate coil springs and telescopic dampers. Anti-roll bar..

Steering: Rack and pinion. Power assistance: standard.

Brakes: Discs front, drums rear, servo-assisted.

Tyres: 185/70 SR 13.   **Fuel tank:** 11.9 Imp. gall (54 litres).

Dimensions: Length 173.9 in (4416 mm), width 67.6 in (1716 mm), height 53.6 in (1362 mm), wheelbase 101.5 in (2579 mm).

Unladen weight: 2204 lb (1000 kg).

Performance *Autocar* test: Maximum speed 98 mph (158 km/h); 0 to 60 mph (100 km/h) 14.7 sec. Fuel consumption at constant 75 mph (120 km/h): 30.0 mpg; overall test, 30.2 mpg.

Features: Competitively priced for a five-seater four-door saloon with good accommodation. Body design by Giugiaro of Turin. Choice of three levels of trim and equipment—L, SL and GSL.

JAGUAR (GB) XJ Sovereign 4.2

Identity: This is likely to be the last appearance of the XJ in this form, with replacement model due 1985. Sovereign became a Jaguar name, instead of Daimler, in 1983, indicating higher trim level. Standard XJ6 3.4 and 4.2 continue. Sovereign spec. available only for 4.2 and V12.

Engine: Front-mounted longitudinal six-cylinder with twin ohc, chain-driven. Alloy head. Bosch L-Jetronic fuel injection. Bore 92.1 mm, stroke 106 mm; capacity 4235 cc. Power 202 bhp (150.5 kW) at 6000 rpm; torque 227 lb ft (314 Nm) at 1500 rpm. Compression 8.7-to-1.

Transmission: Rear-wheel drive; three-speed automatic transmission standard (Borg Warner 66). Top gear speed at 1000 rpm: 24.8 mph (39.9 km/h).

Suspension: Front, independent, wishbones and coil springs; telescopic dampers. Anti-roll bar. Rear, trailing arms, wishbones and fixed length drive shafts; dual coil spring and telescopic damper units each side.

Steering: Rack and pinion. Power assistance: standard.

Brakes: Vented discs front and inboard (solid) rear, servo-assisted.

Tyres: 205/70 VR 15. **Fuel tanks:** 20 (total) Imp. gall (91 litres).

Dimensions: Length 195.2 in (4959 mm), width 69.7 in (1770 mm), height 54 in (1377 mm), wheelbase 112.8 in (2866 mm).

Unladen weight: 3978 lb (1805 kg).

Performance *Autocar* test: Maximum speed 127 mph (204 km/h); 0 to 60 mph (100 km/h) 10.0 sec. Fuel consumption at·constant 75 mph (120 km/h): 23.7 mpg; overall test, 16.8 mpg.

Features: Superbly quiet and refined performance saloon. Sovereign version adds alloy wheels, trip computer, air conditioning, and electric remote adjust mirrors, plus carpeted boot and other refinements.

Identity: Two new models to supplement existing XJS HE launched Motorfair 1983 featured the entirely new AJ6 engine. Hardtop (XJ-S 3.6) looks like the HE except for lettering on back, but Cabriolet also features removable Targa roof panels and folding rear hood.

Engine: Front-mounted in-line six-cylinder with twin ohc and 24 valves. All-alloy construction with dry cast iron liners. Bore, 91 mm, stroke 92 mm; capacity 3590 cc. Power 225 bhp (168 kW) at 5300 rpm; torque 240 lb ft (325 Nm) at 4000 rpm. Comp. 9.6-to-1.

Transmission: Rear-wheel drive; five-speed manual gearbox; no automatic option for six-cylinder model. Final drive 3.54-to-1. Top gear speed at 1000 rpm: 28.9 mph (46.5 km/h).

Suspension: Front, independent, semi-trailing wishbones with anti-dive geometry; coil springs and telescopic dampers. Anti-roll bar. Rear, independent, lower transverse wishbones and drive shafts acting as upper links. Twin concentric coil spring and damper units each side.

Steering: Rack and pinion. Power assistance: standard.

Brakes: Vented discs front, solid discs rear, servo-assisted.

Tyres: 215/70 VR 15.   **Fuel tank:** 20.0 Imp. gall (91 litres).

Dimensions: Length 187.6 in (4764 mm), width 70.6 in (1793 mm), height 49.7 in (1261 mm), wheelbase 102 in (2591 mm).

Unladen weight: 3660 lb (1660 kg).

Performance *Autocar* test: Maximum speed 141 mph (227 km/h); 0 to 60 mph (100 km/h) 7.4 sec. Fuel consumption at constant 75 mph (120 km/h) 29.4 mpg; overall test, 17.6 mpg.

Features: 'Starfish' alloy wheels; leather trim for seats, console and door panels. Two-seater only, with concealed lockable bins beneath rear deck. Very neat and simple-to-operate hood mechanism.

LADA (SU)

Identity: Rugged cross-country vehicle, identifiable by the unusual positioning of side and indicator lamps above the headlamps. Not a very pleasant vehicle to drive, but inexpensive for a four-wheel-drive estate car.

Engine: Front-mounted four-cylinder with chain-driven overhead camshaft. Alloy cylinder-head. Bore 79 mm, stroke 80 mm; capacity 1569 cc. Power 77 bhp (57.5 kW) at 5400 rpm; torque 89 lb ft (123 Nm) at 3200 rpm. Compression 8.5-to-1.

Transmission: Four-wheel drive; four-speed gearbox with low ratio transfer box. Final drive 4.3-to-1. Top gear speed at 1000 rpm: 15.3 mph (24.6 km/h).

Suspension: Front, live axle, wishbones and coil springs; telescopic dampers. Anti-roll bar. Rear, live axle, longitudinal links and Panhard rod; coil springs and telescopic dampers.

Steering: Worm and roller. Power assistance: not available.

Brakes: Discs front, drums rear, servo-assisted.

Tyres: 6.95/16.   **Fuel tank:** 9.9 Imp. gall (40 litres).

Dimensions: Length 146 in (3708 mm), width 66 in (1676 mm), height 64.5 in (1638 mm), wheelbase 86.5 in (2197 mm).

Unladen weight: 2535 lb (1150 kg).

Performance *Autocar* test: Maximum speed 77 mph (124 km/h); 0 to 60 mph (100 km/h) 22.4 sec. Fuel consumption, 23.3 mpg (at constant 75 mph (120 km/h)); overall test, 20.0 mpg.

Features: Crude but durable and practical interior. Two-door body with opening back. Good cross-country performance. For a long time the Niva was available in UK only with lhd, but rhd examples are now offered. Headlamps wash/wipe and better throttle control introduced for 1985.

LANCIA (I)　　　　　　　　　　Delta HF Turbo

Identity: The latest and top performance version of the Delta, introduced 1984 with neat turbocharger installation. Lancia claim it to be the fastest 1600 cc five-door hatchback on the market. New instrumentation for 1985.

Engine: Front-mounted transverse four-cylinder with twin ohc, Garrett turbocharger, Weber carb. Marelli Microplax electronic ignition. Bore 84 mm, stroke 71.5 mm; capacity 1585 cc. Power 130 bhp (96 kW) at 5600 rpm; torque 138 lb ft (191 Nm) at 3700 rpm. Compression 8.0-to-1.

Transmission: Front-wheel drive; five-speed manual gearbox; no automatic option. Top gear speed at 1000 rpm: 20.9 mph (33.6 km/h).

Suspension: Front, independent, MacPherson struts, coil springs, telescopic dampers. Anti-roll bar. Rear, independent, MacPherson struts, coil springs and telescopic dampers. Anti-roll bar.

Steering: Rack and pinion. Power assistance: not available.

Brakes: Discs front and rear, servo-assisted.

Tyres: 176/65 R 13.　　　**Fuel tank:** 9.9 Imp. gall (45 litres).

Dimensions: Length 153.5 in (3895 mm), width 64 in (1620 mm), height 54.3 in (1380 mm), wheelbase 97.4 in (2475 mm).

Unladen weight: 2205 lb (1000 kg).

Performance *Autocar* test: Maximum speed 121 mph (195 km/h); 0 to 60 mph (100 km/h) 8.2 sec. Fuel consumption at constant 75 mph (120 km/h): 30.4 mpg; overall test, 25.6 mpg.

Features: Very quick hatchback. Turbocharger has air-to-air heat exchanger. Gearbox is a close-ratio ZF. New for 1985 is the 'Bar graph' instrumentation. Executive pack available which includes steel sliding sunroof, central locking and electric front window lifts.

Identity: Impressive new model range to restore Lancia's standing in the upper segment of the market, launched Turin 1984—on UK market early 1985. Choice of four engines in some markets—2-litre with and without turbo, V6 2.8-litre (PRV engine), and 2½-litre turbo diesel four-cylinder. Both i.e. (injection electronic) and diesel are impressive.

Engine: Front-mounted transverse four-cylinder with belt-driven ohc, twin-counter-rotating balance shafts, and Bosch L-Jetronic injection. Bore 84 mm, stroke 90 mm; capacity 1995 cc. Power 165 bhp (122 kW) at 5500 rpm; torque 184 lb ft (255 Nm) at 2500 rpm. Compression 8.0-to-1.

Transmission: Front-wheel drive; five-speed manual gearbox; three-speed AP automatic transmission optional for non-turbo and V6. Top gear speed at 1000 rpm: 24.7 mph (39.8 km/h).

Suspension: Front, independent, MacPherson struts and coil springs; telescopic dampers. Anti-roll bar. Rear, independent, MacPherson struts and transverse dampers. Self-levelling optional.

Steering: Rack and pinion. Power assistance: standard.

Brakes: Discs front and rear, servo-assisted.

Tyres: 195/60 VR 14.   **Fuel tank:** 15.4 Imp. gall (70 litres).

Dimensions: Length 180.7 in (4590 mm), width 69 in (1755 mm), height 56.4 in (1433 mm), wheelbase 104.7 in (2660 mm).

Unladen weight: 2535 lb (1150 kg).

Performance (Works): Maximum speed 136 mph (218 km/h); 0 to 60 mph (100 km/h) 7.2 sec. Fuel consumption at constant 75 mph (120 km/h): 33.6 mpg.

Features: Very pleasing car, with excellent response, first-class road manners and high level of equipment.

Identity: Geneva 1983 saw introduction of the One Ten, the new model so called because of its 110 in. wheelbase. The shorter version is logically called the 90. Available with either 2.3-litre petrol or 2.5-litre diesel engine. Permanent four-wheel drive and dual range five-speed transmission.

Engine: Front-mounted longitudinal four-cylinder with pushrod ohv. Twin-choke Weber carb. Bore 90.47 mm, stroke 88.9 mm; capacity 2286 cc. Power 74 bhp (55 kW) at 4000 rpm; torque 120 lb ft (163 Nm) at 2000 rpm. Compression 8-to-1.

Transmission: Permanent four-wheel drive; five-speed manual gearbox; dual range transfer box. Lockable centre diff. Top gear speed at 1000 rpm: 18 mph (29 km/h).

Suspension: Front, single rate coil springs, live beam axle, double acting telescopic dampers, Panhard rod. Rear, A-frame, live beam axle, single rate coil springs, double acting telescopic dampers.

Steering: Worm and roller. Power assistance: not available.

Brakes: Discs front, drums rear, servo-assisted.

Tyres: 7.50-16.   **Fuel tank:** 17.5 Imp. gall (79.5 litres).

Dimensions: Length 152.9 in (3883 mm), width 70.5 in (1790 mm), height 77.6 in (1972 mm), wheelbase 92.9in (2360 mm).

Unladen weight: 5291 lb (2400 kg).

Performance (Works): Maximum speed 70 mph (110 km/h). Fuel consumption at constant 56 mph (90 km/h): 22.9 mpg.

Features: Wide variety of body styles and equipment available for this go-anywhere vehicle. Interior trim now far less spartan; reclining cloth-covered seats and even carpets now available.

LAND ROVER (GB)　　　Range Rover Vogue

Identity: Latest stage in the steady improvement of Range Rover came June 1984, with further upgrading of trim and equipment, and top luxury model was given the name Vogue, previously used before for special editions. Identity feature is deletion of quarter vents in front doors.

Engine: Front-mounted longitudinal V8-cylinder with all-alloy construction. Pushrod ohv and hydraulic tappets. 2 Stromberg carbs. Bore 88.9 mm, stroke 71.1 mm; capacity 3528 cc. Power 125 bhp (93 kW) at 4000 rpm; torque 185 lb ft (258 Nm) at 2500 rpm. Compression 9.4-to-1.

Transmission: Four-wheel drive; five-speed manual gearbox; three-speed automatic optional. Transfer gearbox gives 1.19-to-1 high ratio, 3.32 low. Top gear speed at 1000 rpm: 25.8 mph (41.5 km/h).

Suspension: Front, live axle on radius arms and Panhard rod; long-travel coil springs and telescopic dampers. Rear, live axle on trailing links with central A-bracket location; coil springs and telescopic dampers. Boge self-levelling strut.

Steering: Recirculating ball. Power assistance: standard.

Brakes: Discs front and rear, servo-assisted.

Tyres: 205-16 M + S.　　**Fuel tank:** 18 Imp. gall (82 litres).

Dimensions: Length 176 in (4470 mm), width 67.7 in (1718 mm), height 70 in (1778 mm), wheelbase 102 in (2591 mm).

Unladen weight: 4163 lb (1892 kg).

Performance *Autocar* test: Maximum speed 96 mph (154 km/h); 0 to 60 mph (100 km/h) 14.4 sec. Fuel consumption, overall test, 15.4 mpg.

Features: Most significant improvement in June 1984 was provision for the seats to have recline adjustment; previously they were fixed.

LINCOLN (USA)

Identity: Last year, this famous American luxury saloon was re-launched in new and more compact design, and this continues for 1985 as do the engine options: V8 5-litre injection unit is standard, with the 2.4-litre turbocharged diesel available. The Continental LSC remains the performance version with firmer suspension.

Engine: Front-mounted longitudinal V8-cylinder with hydraulic tappets and fuel injection. Bore 101.6 mm, stroke 76.2 mm; capacity 4942 cc. Power 145 bhp (108 kW) at 3600 rpm; torque 240 lb ft (332 Nm) at 2200 rpm. Compression 8.4-to-1.

Transmission: Rear-wheel drive; four-speed automatic transmission with overdrive top gear. Speed at 1000 rpm: 35 mph (56.3 km/h).

Suspension: Front, independent, modified MacPherson struts, air springs and automatic self-levelling. Telescopic gas-filled dampers. Anti-roll bar. Rear, live axle on trailing arms with air spring units. Telescopic gas-filled dampers. Anti-roll bar.

Steering: Rack and pinion. Power assistance: standard.

Brakes: Discs front and rear, servo-assisted.

Tyres: P215/70 R-15.   **Fuel tank:** 18.6 Imp. gall (84 litres).

Dimensions: Length 201.2 in (5110 mm), width 73.6 in (1869 mm), height 54.8 in (1392 mm), wheelbase 108.6 in (2758 mm).

Unladen weight: 3750 lb (1701 kg).

Performance (est.): Maximum speed 110 mph (177 km/h). Fuel consumption: 20 mpg (est.).

Features: Major change for 1985 is the addition of electronically controlled four-wheel Anti-Lock Brake System. Inside there are new front seats with a six-way power adjustment system. Equipment has also been improved for all models.

LOTUS (GB)   **Eclat Excel**

Identity: Attractive 2 + 2 sports car gets new body styling changes for 1985, including restyled front bumpers, new Lotus badging, rear window increased in width and depth and neat rear aerofoil. Mechanically the same as last year. New interior instrumentation.

Engine: Front-mounted in-line four-cylinder with four valves per cylinder. Alloy head and block. Belt driven twin ohc. Bore 95.3 mm, stroke 76.2 mm; capacity 2174 cc. Power 160 bhp (119 kW) at 6500 rpm; torque 160 lb ft (221 Nm) at 4000 rpm. Compression 9.4-to-1.

Transmission: Rear-wheel drive; five-speed manual gearbox; automatic transmission optional. Top gear speed at 1000 rpm: 21.2 mph (34 km/h).

Suspension: Front, independent, wishbones and coil springs, telescopic dampers. Anti-roll bar. Rear, independent, wishbones and coil springs; telescopic dampers.

Steering: Rack and pinion. Power assistance: optional.

Brakes: Ventilated discs front and rear, servo-assisted.

Tyres: 205/60 VR 14.   **Fuel tank:** 14.7 Imp. gall (67 litres).

Dimensions: Length 172.3 in (4376 mm), width 71.5 in (1816 mm), height 40.4 in (1207 mm), wheelbase 97.8 in (2483 mm).

Unladen weight: 2205 lb (1135 kg).

Performance *Autocar* test: Maximum speed 130 mph (210 km/h); 0 to 60 mph (100 km/h) 7.1 sec. Fuel consumption at constant 75 mph (120 km/h): 29.4 mpg; overall test, 19.5 mpg.

Features: Glass fibre body, pop-up headlamps. New alloy wheels distinguish 1985 model. High standard of performance and superb handling. Many Toyota components used in Excel's running gear.

LOTUS (GB)

Esprit S3

Identity: Revised version of Lotus Esprit introduced Birmingham 1984. Body mainly as before, but revised tailgate has recess for easier lift and entry. Revised paint finish and new decals. Turbo version also available. Bumpers and mirror housings in body colour identify 1985 model.

Engine: Mid-mounted longitudinal four-cylinder with twin ohc and 4 valves per cylinder. All alloy construction. Twin Dellorto carbs. Bore 95.3 mm, stroke 76.2 mm; capacity 2174 cc. Power 160 bhp (119 kW) at 6500 rpm; torque 160 lb ft (221 Nm) at 5000 rpm. Comp. 9.4-to-1.

Transmission: Rear-wheel drive; five-speed manual gearbox; no automatic transmission option. Top gear speed at 1000 rpm: 22.7 mph (36.5 km/h).

Suspension: Front, independent, upper and lower wishbones and coil springs with coaxial twin-tube telescopic dampers. Anti-roll bar. Rear, independent, transverse links with radius arms; coil springs and telescopic dampers.

Steering: Rack and pinion. Power assistance: not available.

Brakes: Vented discs front, solid discs rear, servo-assisted.

Tyres: 195/60 VR 15 (front), 235/60 VR 15 (rear).   **Fuel tank:** 14.8 Imp. gall (67 litres).

Dimensions: Length 165 in (4191 mm), width 73 in (1854 mm), height 44 in (1118 mm), wheelbase 96 in (2438 mm).

Unladen weight: 2690 lb (1220 kg).

Performance *Autocar* test: Maximum speed 130 mph (209 km/h); 0 to 60 mph (100 km/h) 7.3 sec. Fuel consumption at constant 75 mph (120 km/h): 24.1 mpg; overall test, 23.2 mpg.

Features: Detail improvements 1984 brought larger boot, trimmed with carpet, and provision for housing optional detachable sunroof.

LOTUS (GB)   Etna

Identity: Undisputed star of the 1984 British Motor Show, where it was unveiled, the Etna is a 180 mph supercar designed by Giugiaro and powered by the new Lotus V8 engine. At the Show it was decided that the Etna would also go into production, hopefully in 1988.

Engine: Mid-mounted 90 deg. V8-cylinder with double overhead cams per bank. Four valves per cylinder. Bore 95.29 mm, stroke 70.30 mm; capacity 3998 cc. Power 330 bhp (246 kW) at 6500 rpm; torque 294 lb ft (399 Nm) at 5500 rpm. Compression 11.2-to-1.

Transmission: Rear-wheel drive. Continuously variable ratio, microprocessor controlled with programmable lock-up mode.

Suspension: Fully active, computer controlled. Variable synthesized spring and damper characteristics with hydraulic activation.

Steering: Rack and pinion. Power assistance: standard.

Brakes: Ventilated discs front and rear, servo-assisted, with ABS.

Tyres: F:215/50-15; R:235/50-16.   **Fuel tank:** 20 Imp. gall (90 litres).

Dimensions: Length 168 in (4268 mm), width 73 in (1844 mm), height 45 in (1143 mm), wheelbase 99 in (2515 mm).

Unladen weight: 2600 lb (1182 kg).

Performance (est.): Maximum speed 182 mph (290 km/h); 0 to 60 mph (100 km/h) 4.3 sec.

Features: A fantastic supercar, brimming with features, including computer-controlled suspension. Anti-lock braking. CVT transmission. Brand new V8 engine which Lotus say is capable of 600 bhp if turbocharged.

MARCOS (GB) Mantula

Identity: A well-established name in the world of kit cars, Marcos was brought back into public attention by taking a stand at Birmingham 1984 to show the Mantula, introduced in the previous year. Mantula has the Rover V8 engine. Other Marcos models look much the same.

Engine: Front-mounted longitudinal V8-cylinder with alloy construction. Dry cylinder liners. Pushrod valve gear with hydraulic tappets. 2 Solex carbs. Fuel injection available. Bore 88.9 mm, stroke 71 mm; capacity 3528 cc. Power 155 bhp (114 kW) at 5200 rpm; torque 195 lb ft (269 Nm) at 2500 rpm. Compression 9.3-to-1.

Transmission: Rear-wheel drive; five-speed manual gearbox; limited slip differential optional. Top gear speed at 1000 rpm: 29.6 mph (47.6 km/h).

Suspension: Front, independent, wishbones and coil springs; telescopic dampers. Anti-roll bar. Rear, live axle on semi-elliptical leaf springs; telescopic dampers.

Steering: Rack and pinion. Power assistance: not available.

Brakes: Vented discs front, drums rear, servo-assisted.

Tyres: 195/65 HR 375.   **Fuel tank:** 10.5 Imp. gall (48 litres).

Dimensions: Length 163.5 in (4153 mm), width 62.5 in (1588 mm), height 42.5 in (1080 mm), wheelbase 89.5 in (2273 mm).

Unladen weight: 1874 lb (850 kg).

Performance (Works): Maximum speed 160 mph (257 km/h); 0 to 60 mph (100 km/h) 6 sec. No fuel consumption data quoted by manufacturers; est. 28 mpg.

Features: Various stages of kits are available, and many buyers obtain major components from scrapped cars, so suspension and other details may vary.

Identity: Only a concept car, and one still far from becoming a production possibility, but the MX-02 introduces many new thoughts on car design for the future. Most fascinating features are key-less entry by pushbutton digits to secret code, navigational aid with cathode ray tube, and four-wheel steering. Low drag body with Cd factor of only 0.22.

Engine: Front-mounted in-line four-cylinder with twin overhead camshafts, 16 valves, and electronic fuel injection. Variable valve timing, and dual induction system. Bore 77 mm, stroke 69.6 mm; capacity 1296 cc. Power 100 bhp (75 kW) at 6800 rpm; torque 87 lb ft (120 Nm) at 3600 rpm.

Transmission: Front-wheel drive; automatic transmission, with finger-tip control.

Suspension: Front, independent, with automatic control of damper settings. Suspension adjustable by finger switches within reach of driver's hands on wheel.

Steering: All four wheels steer, and amount of rear steering is computer-controlled according to vehicle speed. At low speeds, rear wheels turn in opposite direction from front ones, giving turning circle of only 14 ft (4.3 m).

Brakes: Discs front, drums rear, servo-assisted, with anti-lock control.

Features: Low-drag body in conjunction with high-efficiency engine claimed to give exceptional fuel economy; but the project is still very much in the sphere of advanced research. The significant development of four-wheel steering is being researched in a Mazda 626, and would offer much greater manoeuvrability, since the car will almost move sideways when the low-speed mode, turning rear wheels in the opposite direction from the front ones, is selected.

Identity: Replacement for previous mid-range model, introduced Japan September 1982, and on British market May 1983. New concept with transverse engine and front drive. Choice of 1600 or 2000 engine and saloon or hatchback body, each with four side doors; also stylish two-door coupé, with 2000 engine only. Details for 1600 LX follow.

Engine: Front-mounted transverse four-cylinder with alloy head, cast iron block. Belt-driven ohc. Breakerless ignition. Bore 81 mm, stroke 77 mm; capacity 1587 cc. Power 81 bhp (60 kW) at 5500 rpm; torque 88 lb ft (122 Nm) at 4000 rpm. Compression 8.6-to-1.

Transmission: Front-wheel drive; five-speed manual gearbox; three speed automatic optional. Top gear speed at 1000 rpm: 21.0 mph (33.8 km/h).

Suspension: Front, independent, MacPherson struts; coil springs and telescopic dampers. Anti-roll bar. Rear, independent, twin trapezoidal links; coil springs and telescopic dampers. Anti-roll bar.

Steering: Rack and pinion. Power assistance: optional.

Brakes: Discs front, drums rear, servo-assisted.

Tyres: 165 SR 13.   **Fuel tank:** 13 Imp. gall (60 litres).

Dimensions: Length 174.4 in (4430 mm), width 66.5 in (1690 mm), height 55 in (1395 mm), wheelbase 98.8 in (2510 mm).

Unladen weight: 2304 lb (1045 kg).

Performance *Autocar* test: Maximum speed 102 mph (164 km/h); 0 to 60 mph (100 km/h) 12.3 sec. Fuel consumption at constant 75 mph (120 km/h): 36.7 mpg; overall test, 30.6 mpg.

Features: Easy car to drive, with smooth engine and pleasant gear change. Finger-tip switches within easy reach of wheel. Good range of equipment; amusing musical tones warn driver of such things as lights left on or belts not fastened. Dampers electronically adjustable.

Identity: Despite all the problems of the past, Mazda persisted with the Wankel rotary engine, and use it to power their sleekly styled two-door coupé with opening rear hatch. Close-coupled 2 + 2 seat capacity, and considerable sporting appeal.

Engine: Front-mounted twin-rotor Wankel of die-cast alloy construction, with steel liners. Breakerless ignition; Nippon carburettor. Chamber capacity, 573 cc. Equivalent engine capacity 2292 cc. Power, 115 bhp (86 kW) at 6000 rpm; torque 112 lb ft (155 Nm) at 4000 rpm. Compression 9.4-to-1.

Transmission: Rear-wheel drive; five-speed manual gearbox (no automatic version). Hypoid bevel final drive, 3.909-to-1. Top gear speed at 1000 rpm: 21.0 mph (33.8 km/h).

Suspension: Front, independent, MacPherson struts, coil springs and telescopic dampers. Anti-roll bar. Rear, live-axle on trailing arms, with Watt linkage. Coil springs and telescopic dampers. Anti-roll bar.

Steering: Recirculating ball. Power assistance: not available.

Brakes: Discs front and rear, servo-assisted.

Tyres: 185/70 HR 13.   **Fuel tank:** 12.1 Imp. gall (55 litres).

Dimensions: Length 170 in (4323 mm), width 66 in (1675 mm), height 49.6 in (1260 mm), wheelbase 95.3 in (2420 mm).

Unladen weight: 2352 lb (1068 kg).

Performance *Autocar* test: Maximum speed 125 mph (201 km/h); 0 to 60 mph (100 km/h) 8.6 sec. Fuel consumption at constant 75 mph (120 km/h): 28.0 mpg; overall test, 22.0 mpg.

Features: Slightly vague steering, but otherwise a pleasant car to drive, with wonderfully smooth engine behaviour. Well-equipped, with electric window lifts and removable glass sunroof.

MERCEDES-BENZ (D) 190D

Identity: Additions to 190 range at Frankfurt 1983 were the spectacularly fast 190E 2.3-16V, and the new diesel version. The diesel became available on UK market at Birmingham 1984, and features total encapsulation of the engine to keep the external noise level down.

Engine: Front-mounted longitudinal four-cylinder with chain-driven ohc and hydraulic tappets. Single belt drive for auxiliaries. Bore 87 mm, stroke 84 mm; capacity 1997 cc. Power 71 bhp (53 kW) at 4600 rpm; torque 89 lb ft (123 Nm) at 2800 rpm. Compression 22-to-1.

Transmission: Rear-wheel drive; four-speed manual gearbox; five-speed manual or four-speed automatic are options. Top gear speed at 1000 rpm: 22.3 mph (35.9 km/h).

Suspension: Front, independent, MacPherson struts; coil springs (separate from struts) and gas-filled telescopic dampers. Anti-roll bar. Rear, independent, ingenious five-link wheel location each side with anti-dive/anti-squat links; coil springs and gas-filled telescopic dampers. Anti-roll bar.

Steering: Recirculating ball, with varying ratio. Power assistance: optional.

Brakes: Discs front and rear, servo-assisted.

Tyres: 175/70 R 14.   **Fuel tank:** 12.1 Imp. gall (55 litres).

Dimensions: Length 174 in (4420 mm), width 66 in (1678 mm), height 54.4 in (1383 mm), wheelbase 105 in (2665 mm).

Unladen weight: 2380 lb (1080 kg).

Performance *Autocar* test: Maximum speed 98 mph (158 km/h); 0 to 60 mph (100 km/h) 15.9 sec. Fuel consumption at constant 75 mph (120 km/h): 40.9 mpg; overall test, 30.8 mpg.

Features: Equipment and finish largely as petrol 190. Good ride and handling.

MERCEDES-BENZ (D)

190E 2.3 16V

Identity: Performance version of 190 range, which set three international speed endurance records in 1983, covering 25,000 miles at just under 155 mph. Production started 1984, and car expected to become available in UK early 1985. High efficiency 16-valve engine.

Engine: Front-mounted longitudinal four-cylinder with twin ohc and four valves per cylinder. Bosch fuel injection. Alloy head. Bore 95.5 mm, stroke 80.3 mm; capacity 2299 cc. Power 185 bhp (138 kW) at 6000 rpm; torque 174 lb ft (240 Nm) at 4500 rpm. Compression 10.5-to-1.

Transmission: Rear-wheel drive; five-speed manual gearbox; closer ratios than in standard 190 and 190E. No automatic option. Top gear speed at 1000 rpm: 23.5 mph (37.8 km/h).

Suspension: Front, independent, MacPherson struts; coil springs separate from struts; telescopic dampers. Anti-roll bar. Rear, independent, five-link system with anti-squat/anti-dive links; coil springs and telescopic dampers. Anti-roll bar. Self-levelling standard.

Steering: Recirculating ball. Power assistance: standard.

Brakes: Vented discs front, solid discs rear, servo-assisted.

Tyres: 205/55 VR 15.   **Fuel tank:** 12.1 Imp. gall (55 litres).

Dimensions: Length 174 in (4420 mm), width 66 in (1678 mm), height 54.4 in (1383 mm), wheelbase 105 in (2665 mm).

Unladen weight: 2380 lb (1080 kg).

Performance (Works): Maximum speed 143 mph (230 km/h); 0 to 60 mph (100 km/h) 8 sec. Fuel consumption at constant 75 mph (120 km/h): 31.4 mpg.

Features: Body embellishments to aid aerodynamics, and spoiler wing on boot, give instant recognition from ordinary 190 models.

Identity: Called W124, new body style similar to 190 launched December 1984, in seven-model line-up. Three diesel engines with 4, 5 and 6 cylinders, plus two four-cylinder and two six-cylinder petrol units. 300E is top model of the range—a fast, safe and eminently satisfying car. Three bright stripes across radiator grille give instant recognition.

Engine: Front-mounted longitudinal six-cylinder with single ohc, valves in V formation. Bosch KE Jetronic fuel injection. Bore 88.5 mm, stroke 80.3 mm; capacity 2962 cc. Power 190 bhp (140 kW) at 5600 rpm; torque 188 lb ft (260 Nm) at 4250 rpm. Compression 10.0-to-1.

Transmission: Rear-wheel drive; five-speed manual gearbox; four-speed automatic transmission optional. Top gear speed at 1000 rpm: 22.3 mph (35.9 km/h).

Suspension: Front, independent, wishbones and struts. Coil spring separate from strut; telescopic dampers. Anti-roll bar. Rear, independent, five-link location; coil springs and telescopic dampers. Anti-roll bar.

Steering: Recirculating ball. Power assistance: standard.

Brakes: Discs front and rear, servo-assisted.

Tyres: 195/65 VR 15.   **Fuel tank:** 15.4 Imp. gall (70 litres).

Dimensions: Length 186.6 in (4740 mm), width 68.5 in (1740 mm), height 57 in (1446 mm), wheelbase 110 in (2800 mm).

Unladen weight: 2954 lb (1340 kg).

Performance (Works): Maximum speed 143 mph (230 km/h); 0 to 60 mph (100 km/h) 7.9 sec. Fuel consumption at constant 75 mph (120 km/h): 34.0 mpg.

Features: Low drag body and efficient engine give a remarkable combination of performance with economy. Wide range of equipment.

MERCEDES-BENZ (D)

380SEC

Identity: Not the top model in the Mercedes two-door coupé range but a very popular choice, giving remarkable combination of performance with comfort, space, style and even economy.

Engine: Front-mounted V8-cylinder with aluminium block and heads; two overhead camshafts; electronic ignition and injection. Bore 88 mm, stroke 79 mm; capacity 3839 cc. Power 204 bhp (152 kW) at 5250 rpm; torque 232 lb ft (321 Nm) at 3250 rpm. Compression 9.4-to-1.

Transmission: Rear-wheel drive; four-speed automatic by Daimler-Benz, with exceptionally high gearing for economy. Automatic kick-down to third right up to 110 mph. Top gear speed at 1000 rpm: 28.5 mph (45.9 km/h).

Suspension: Front, independent, wishbones and coil springs, tele-scopic dampers; anti-roll bar. Rear, independent, semi-trailing arms, coil springs; telescopic dampers, anti-roll bar.

Steering: Recirculating ball. Power assistance: standard.

Brakes: Discs front and rear, servo-assisted, internally vented.

Tyres: 205/70 VR 14.   **Fuel tank:** 19.8 Imp. gall (90 litres).

Dimensions: Length 193 in (4910 mm), width 72 in (1828 mm), height 55.4 in (1406 mm), wheelbase 112 in (2850 mm).

Unladen weight: 3507 lb (1592 kg).

Performance *Autocar* test: Maximum speed 131 mph (211 km/h); 0 to 60 mph (100 km/h) 9.1 sec. Fuel consumption, 26.2 mpg (at constant 75 mph (120 km/h)); overall test, 19.9 mpg.

Features: Lavish standard equipment including sunroof with electric control, electric window lifts and central locking; air conditioning extra. Very high gearing was adopted for this and other S-class models economy.

MERCEDES-BENZ (D)

Identity: Original appearance of the Mercedes open two-seater sports with this body was in 1971, but this was the first car to be fitted with the new all-alloy V8, launched as the 500SL at Geneva 1980. Superbly refined and fast convertible.

Engine: Front-mounted V8-cylinder with chain-driven ohc each bank; alloy heads and block. Bosch K-Jetronic injection. Bore 96.5 mm, stroke 85 mm; capacity 4973 cc. Power 228 bhp (170 kW) at 4750 rpm; torque 292 lb ft (405 Nm) at 3200 rpm. Compression 9.2-to-1.

Transmission: Rear-wheel drive; Daimler-Benz four-speed automatic. Very high final drive ratio, 2.24-to-1. Limited slip-diff. Top gear speed at 1000 rpm: 33.6 mph (54.0 km/h).

Suspension: Front, independent, wishbones and coil springs; telescopic dampers. Anti-roll bar. Rear, independent, semi-trailing arms; coil springs and telescopic dampers. Anti-roll bar.

Steering: Recirculating ball. Power assistance: standard.

Brakes: Vented discs front, solid discs rear, servo-assisted.

Tyres: 205/70 VR 14.   **Fuel tank:** 18.7 Imp. gall (85 litres).

Dimensions: Length 172.8 in (4389 mm), width 70.5 in (1790 mm), height 51.2 in (1300 mm), wheelbase 96.6 in (2455 mm).

Unladen weight: 3395 lb (1540 kg).

Performance (Works): Maximum speed 137 mph (220 km/h); 0 to 60 mph (100 km/h) 8.0 sec. Fuel consumption, 24.6 mpg (at constant 75 mph (120 km/h)).

Features: Excellent sealing of hood and frameless glass side windows. Hood folds into a well, and is covered by rigid, hinged top. Hardtop available. Well finished and very fully equipped.

MERCURY (USA)

Cougar

Identity: The sporting, mid-sized Mercury is the Cougar. For 1985 it has a new grille, tail-lamps and wheel covers. Available only as a two-door coupé, the Cougar has either the 2.3-litre turbocharged, V6 3.8-litre fuel injected engine, or 5.0-litre V8 with fuel injection.

Engine: Front-mounted longitudinal four-cylinder with belt-driven ohc. Hydraulic tappets. Electronic fuel injection and Garrett turbocharger. Bore 96.04 mm, stroke 79.4 mm; capacity 2301 cc. Power 145 bhp (108 kW) at 4600 rpm; torque 176 lb ft (244 Nm) at 3600 rpm. Compression 9.0-to-1.

Transmission: Rear-wheel drive; five-speed manual gearbox; three-speed automatic optional. Top gear speed at 1000 rpm: 25 mph (40.2 km/h).

Suspension: Front, independent, MacPherson struts, coil springs bearing on to lower arms; telescopic dampers. Anti-roll bar. Rear, live axle on four locating links; coil springs and telescopic dampers. Anti-roll bar.

Steering: Rack and pinion. Power assistance: standard.

Brakes: Discs front, drums rear, servo-assisted.

Tyres: 195/75 R 14.   **Fuel tank:** 15.0 Imp. gall (68 litres).

Dimensions: Length 197.6 in (5020 mm), width 71.0 in (1805 mm), height 53.3 in (1355 mm), wheelbase 103.9 in (2640 mm).

Unladen weight: 2987 lb (1355 kg).

Performance (est.): Maximum speed 111 mph (180 km/h). Fuel consumption: 18 mpg (est.).

Features: Three new instrument facias are available for 1985, including a fully electronic version. Standard for the new model year is a split bench front seat. 15 inch wheels are available as an option.

MERCURY (USA) **Marquis**

Identity: Mercury's mid-sized saloon has a new appearance for 1985, revised grille, wide bodyside mouldings and new tail-lamp lenses. Available as a four-door saloon or station wagon, the Marquis has the option of four-cylinder 2.3-litre or V6 3.8-litre engines with fuel injection.

Engine: Front-mounted in line four-cylinder with hydraulic tappets. Carter carb. Bore, 96.04 mm, stroke 79.4 mm; capacity 2301 cc. Power 88 bhp (65.5 kW) at 4000 rpm; torque 122 lb ft (166 Nm) at 2400 rpm. Compression 9.0-to-1.

Transmission: Rear-wheel drive; three-speed Cruise-O-Matic automatic gearbox. Top gear speed at 1000 rpm: 21.3 mph (34.3 km/h).

Suspension: Front, independent, MacPherson struts, coil springs bearing on to lower arms; telescopic dampers. Anti-roll bar. Rear, live axle on four locating links, coil springs and gas-filled telescopic dampers. Anti-roll bar.

Steering: Rack and pinion. Power assistance: standard.

Brakes: Ventilated discs front, drums rear, servo-assisted.

Tyres: 185/75 R 14.　　**Fuel tank:** 13.4 Imp. gall (61 litres).

Dimensions: Length 186.5 in (4990 mm), width 70.9 in (1800 mm), height 53.5 in (1360 mm), wheelbase 105.5 in (2680 mm).

Unladen weight: 2932 lb (1330 kg).

Performance (est.): Maximum speed 87 mph (140 km/h). Fuel consumption: 23.5 mpg (est.).

Features: Inside the Marquis there are new trim, colours and fabrics. A more efficient power steering pump and improved body corrosion protection are also new for 1985.

MG (GB)   Maestro EFi

Identity: Launched Birmingham 1984, this is the top performing Maestro—the MG variant powered by the 2-litre fuel injected engine first introduced in the MG Montego. Electronic digital instrumentation with computer and voice synthesizer. Colour-keyed front grille and door mirrors identify EFi from former 1600.

Engine: Front-mounted transverse four-cylinder with aluminium alloy head, cast iron block. Lucas electronic fuel injection. Bore 84.5 mm, stroke 89 mm; capacity 1994 cc. Power 115 bhp (85.8 kW) at 5500 rpm; torque 134 lb ft (182 Nm) at 2800 rpm. Comp. 9.1-to-1.

Transmission: Front-wheel drive; five-speed manual gearbox; no automatic option of MG. Top gear speed at 1000 rpm: 22.0 mph (35.4 km/h).

Suspension: Front, independent, MacPherson struts and lower arms; coil springs and telescopic dampers. Anti-roll bar. Rear, semi-independent, trailing arms, torsion beam, coil springs; telescopic dampers.

Steering: Rack and pinion. Power assistance: optional.

Brakes: Ventilated discs front, drums rear, servo-assisted.

Tyres: 175 HR 14.   **Fuel tank:** 11.2 Imp. gall (53 litres).

Dimensions: Length 159.5 in (4050 mm), width 66.4 in (1690 mm), height 56.1 in (1420 mm), wheelbase 98.7 in (2510 mm).

Unladen weight: 2249 lb (1020 kg).

Performance (Works): Maximum speed 115 mph (185 km/h); 0 to 60 mph (100 km/h) 8.5 sec. Fuel consumption at constant 75 mph (120 km/h): 34.8 mpg.

Features: Easily distinguishable with MG badging and neat colour-coded pin-stripes along body sides. Lack of chrome trim adds to sporting appearance. Responsive engine, comfortable car to drive.

Identity: Introduced Birmingham 1982, this is the performance version of the Metro, with very neatly engineered turbo installation. Larger alloy wheels than standard MG Metro. Deep black spoiler with cooling inlets for brakes at front, and the work TURBO is lettered on the doors.

Engine: Front-mounted transverse four-cylinder with pushrod ohv. Garrett AiResearch turbocharger. Cast iron head and block. Bore 70.6 mm, stroke 81.3 mm; capacity 1275 cc. Power 93 bhp (70 kW) at 6130 rpm; torque 85 lb ft (118 Nm) at 2650 rpm. Compression 9.4-to-1.

Transmission: Front-wheel drive; four-speed manual gearbox; positioned in engine sump. Final drive 3.21-to-1. Top gear speed at 1000 rpm: 18.6 mph (30 km/h).

Suspension: Front, independent, unequal length links with Hydragas springs and telescopic dampers. Anti-roll bar. Rear, independent, trailing arms; Hydragas springs; integral damping in Hydragas unit. Transverse interconnection of Hydragas units. Anti-roll bar.

Steering: Rack and pinion. Power assistance: not available.

Brakes: Vented discs front, drums rear, servo-assisted.

Tyres: 165/60 VR 13.   **Fuel tank:** 6.5 Imp. gall (29.5 litres).

Dimensions: Length 134.1 in (3403 mm), width 61.6 in (1563 mm), height 53.5 in (1359 mm), wheelbase 88.6 in (2251 mm).

Unladen weight: 1852 lb (840 kg).

Performance *Autocar* test: Maximum speed 110 mph (177 km/h); 0 to 60 mph (100 km/h) 9.4 sec. Fuel consumption at constant 75 mph (120 km/h): 35.1 mpg; overall test, 30.3 mpg.

Features: A much better version of the MG thanks to extra power and higher gearing. LED gauge indicates turbo boost. Grey interior. Sports seats.

MG (GB)

Montego EFi

Identity: Sporting version of the Montego, powered by the 2-litre O-series engine, boosted by Lucas electronic fuel injection. Features include on-board computer with synthesized female voice warning system, MG badges, and digital instruments.

Engine: Front-mounted transverse four-cylinder with aluminium alloy head, cast iron block. Electronic fuel injection. Bore 84.5 mm, stroke 89 mm; capacity 1994 cc. Power 117 bhp (87.2 kW) at 5500 rpm; torque 134 lb ft (182 Nm) at 2800 rpm. Compression 9.1-to-1.

Transmission: Front-wheel drive; five-speed manual gearbox. Top gear speed at 1000 rpm: 20.6 mph (33 km/h).

Suspension: Front, independent, MacPherson struts and lower arms, and coil springs; telescopic dampers. Anti-roll bar. Rear, semi-independent, trailing arms, torsion beam, coil springs, telescopic dampers.

Steering: Rack and pinion. Power assistance: optional.

Brakes: Ventilated discs front, drums rear, servo-assisted.

Tyres: 180/65 HR 365.   **Fuel tank:** 11.2 Imp. gall (53 litres).

Dimensions: Length 175.9 in (4468 mm), width 67.3 in (1710 mm), height 55.9 in (1420 mm), wheelbase 101 in (2565 mm).

Unladen weight: 2300 lb (1043 kg).

Performance *Autocar* test: Maximum speed 114 mph (182 km/h); 0 to 60 mph (100 km/h) 9.6 sec. Fuel consumption at constant 75 mph (120 km/h): 33.5 mpg; overall test, 29.3 mpg.

Features: Lively response, good handling and comfortable ride make the MG Montego an enjoyable car to drive. Matching body colour for grille, front and rear bumpers and minimal brightwork add to sporting look.

MITSUBISHI (J)   Cordia Turbo

Identity: New Colt medium-sized models came on the market in Britain at Birmingham 1982, called Cordia and Tredia. Cordia is the hatchback version, and Tredia the mechanically similar saloon. Each is available with 1597 cc engine, with or without turbo; Tredia also comes with 1410 engine.

Engine: Front-mounted transverse four-cylinder with alloy head and single belt-driven ohc. Aisin twin-choke carb. Bore 76.9 mm, stroke 86 mm; capacity 1597 cc. Power 112 bhp (84 kW) at 5500 rpm; torque 125 lb ft (173 Nm) at 3500 rpm. Compression 8.5-to-1.

Transmission: Front-wheel drive; four-speed manual gearbox; range change lever gives total choice of eight forward ratios. Top gear speed at 1000 rpm: 22.8 mph (36.7 km/h).

Suspension: Front, independent, MacPherson struts; coil springs and telescopic dampers. Anti-roll bar. Rear, independent, trailing arms; coil springs and telescopic dampers.

Steering: Rack and pinion. Power assistance: not available.

Brakes: Vented discs front, drums rear, servo-assisted.

Tyres: 180/70 HR 13.   **Fuel tank:** 11 Imp. gall (50 litres).

Dimensions: Length 168.3 in (4275 mm), width 65.4 in (1600 mm), height 52 in (1320 mm), wheelbase 96.3 in (2445 mm).

Unladen weight: 2149 lb (975 kg).

Performance *Autocar* test: Maximum speed 111 mph (179 km/h); 0 to 60 mph (100 km/h) 9.2 sec. Fuel consumption at constant 75 mph (120 km/h): 34.9 mpg; overall test, 25.2 mpg.

Features: Two-door hatchback body; well-equipped car with radio/cassette and sunroof among wide range of standard equipment. Very responsive engine.

MITSUBISHI (J)   Colt 1600 Turbo

Identity: Colt Cars adopted the company's corporate Mitsubishi name from 1984 in Britain. For the smallest hatchback model in the range, however, the previous Mirage name was dropped and Colt used. The Mitsubishi Colt has new body style for 1985 and is available with 1200, 1500, 1600 Turbo and 1800 diesel engine options.

Engine: Front-mounted transverse four-cylinder with ohc and toothed belt drive. Turbocharger with electronically controlled fuel injection. Knock sensor. Bore 76.9 mm, stroke 86 mm; capacity 1597 cc. Power 123 bhp (92 kW) at 5500 rpm; torque 137.2 lb ft (186 Nm) at 3000 rpm. Compression 7.8-to-1.

Transmission: Front-wheel drive; five-speed manual gearbox; Top gear speed at 1000 rpm: 22.2 mph (35.8 km/h).

Suspension: Front, independent, MacPherson struts, coil springs; telescopic dampers. Anti-roll bar. Rear, independent, MacPherson struts, coil springs; telescopic dampers. Anti-roll bar.

Steering: Rack and pinion. Power assistance: not available.

Brakes: Ventilated discs front, drums rear, servo-assisted.

Tyres: 185/60 HR-14.   **Fuel tank:** 9.9 Imp. gall (45 litres).

Dimensions: Length 152.4 in (3870 mm), width 64.4 in (1635 mm), height 53.5 in (1360 mm), wheelbase 93.7 in (2380 mm).

Unladen weight: 2050 lb (929 kg).

Performance *Autocar* test: Maximum speed 114 mph (183 km/h); 0 to 60 mph (100 km/h) 8.7 sec. Fuel consumption at constant 75 mph (120 km/h): 33.2 mpg; overall test, 23.0 mpg.

Features: Turbo version has front and rear spoilers and side skirts. Impressive acceleration. Light controls, easy to drive. Inside there are sports seats and turbo style steering wheel.

MITSUBISHI (J)   Lancer 1500 GLX

Identity: All-new Lancer range with front-wheel drive was introduced in UK May 1984. Four-door three-box saloon range sharing many components with Colt Hatchback. Three-model UK range starts with 1200 GL, and there are manual or automatic versions of 1500 GLX, plus very impressive 1800 GL diesel.

Engine: Front-mounted transverse four-cylinder with single ohc and counter-rotating balance shafts. Aisin twin-choke carb. Bore 75.5 mm, stroke 82 mm; capacity 1468 cc. Power 73.7 bhp (55 kW) at 5500 rpm; torque 83.3 lb ft (113 Nm) at 4000 rpm. Comp. 9.5-to-1.

Transmission: Front-wheel drive; five-speed manual gearbox; three-speed automatic optional. Top gear speed at 1000 rpm: 24.3 mph (39.0 km/h).

Suspension: Front, independent, MacPherson struts and coil springs; telescopic dampers. Anti-roll bar. Rear, independent, U-shaped trailing arms and coil springs; telescopic dampers. Anti-roll bar.

Steering: Rack and pinion. Power assistance: not available.

Brakes: Ventilated discs front, drums rear, servo-assisted.

Tyres: 155 SR 13.   **Fuel tank:** 9.9 Imp. gall (45 litres).

Dimensions: Length 162.4 in (4125 mm), width 64.4 in (1635 mm), height 53.5 in (1360 mm), wheelbase 93.7 in (2380 mm).

Unladen weight: 1895 lb (860 kg).

Performance (Works): Maximum speed 99 mph (160 km/h). Fuel consumption at constant 75 mph (120 km/h): 38.2 mpg.

Features: Neat body with clean styling and good use of space. Generous equipment on 1500 GLX includes radio, electric front window lifts, remote electric adjustment for door mirrors, central locking, and divided rear seat.

MITSUBISHI (J)   Space Wagon

Identity: The Japanese spearheaded the recent trend for what have been called 'people-carriers'. Mitsubishi's offering is the Space Wagon with its three rows of seats—all forward facing. It comes in manual or automatic form with 1.8-litre engine.

Engine: Front-mounted transverse four-cylinder with ohc and twin counter-rotating balance shafts. Bore 80.6 mm, stroke 86 mm; capacity 1755 cc. Power 88.5 bhp (66 kW) at 5500 rpm; torque 97.4 lb ft (132 Nm) at 4000 rpm. Compression 9.5-to-1.

Transmission: Front-wheel drive; five-speed manual gearbox; three-speed automatic transmission optional.

Suspension: Front, independent, MacPherson struts, coil springs, telescopic dampers. Anti-roll bar. Rear, independent, U-shaped trailing arms, coil springs and variable-rate telescopic dampers.

Steering: Rack and pinion. Power assistance: standard.

Brakes: Ventilated discs front, drums rear, servo-assisted.

Tyres: 165/SR-13.   **Fuel tank:** 11 Imp. gall (50 litres).

Dimensions: Length 169.1 in (4295 mm), width 64.6 in (1640 mm), height 60.0 in (1525 mm), wheelbase 103.3 in (2625 mm).

Unladen weight: 2315 lb (1050 kg).

Performance (est.): Maximum speed 101 mph (162 km/h). Fuel consumption at constant 75 mph (120 km/h): 33.2 mpg.

Features: The Space Wagon will comfortably seat seven in its three rows of forward-facing seats. There are wide-ranging adjustment provisions, or seats can be folded for increased luggage-carrying facility. Well equipped. Central locking is available as an option.

MITSUBISHI (J) Starion

Identity: Impressively styled and sporty-looking four-seater two-door coupé with opening rear window. Pop-up headlamps. Ingenious seat belt arrangement, with inertia reel mounted in doors. Air scoop on bonnet. Energy absorbing bumpers, integral with body at front.

Engine: Front-mounted in-line four-cylinder with electronic fuel injection and Mitsubishi turbocharger. Bore 85 mm, stroke 88 mm; capacity 1997 cc. Power 168 bhp (125 kW) at 5500 rpm; torque 181 lb ft (250 Nm) at 3500 rpm. Compression 7.6-to-1.

Transmission: Rear-wheel drive; five-speed manual gearbox; limited slip diff. Automatic available in some markets (not Britain). Top gear speed at 1000 rpm: 24.4 mph (39.3 km/h).

Suspension: Front, independent, MacPherson struts; coil springs and telescopic dampers. Anti-roll bar. Rear, independent, MacPherson struts and lower links; coil springs and telescopic dampers. Anti-roll bar.

Steering: Recirculating ball. Power assistance: standard.

Brakes: Vented discs front and rear, servo-assisted.

Tyres: 205/70 VR 14.   **Fuel tank:** 16.5 Imp. gall (75 litres).

Dimensions: Length 174 in (4425 mm), width 67 in (1705 mm), height 52 in (1315 mm), wheelbase 96 in (2435 mm).

Unladen weight: 2700 lb (1225 kg).

Performance *Autocar* test: Maximum speed 133 mph (214 km/h); 0 to 60 mph (100 km/h) 7.5 sec. Fuel consumption at constant 75 mph (120 km/h): 29.9 mpg; overall test, 22.1 mpg.

Features: Impressive performance, very safe handling, and excellent brakes. Thoughtful provisions for multiple seat adjustment to suit all shapes of driver, including side bolster adjustment for cushion. Rear seats fold for extra luggage space, but boot space is severely limited. Alloy wheels standard. A remarkably good GT car.

Identity: One of the longest-surviving production cars, the Morgan continues to enjoy stronger demand than the rate of supply from the little Malvern factory can satisfy. Hand-built two-seater with folding hood and detachable sidescreens. Rover V8 engine and five-speed gearbox.

Engine: Front-mounted longitudinal V8-cylinder with alloy heads and block. Twin Zenith-Stromberg carbs. Hydraulic tappets. Bore 88.9 mm, stroke 71.1 mm; capacity 3528 cc. Power 155 bhp (116 kW) at 5250 rpm; torque 193 lb ft (267 Nm) at 2500 rpm. Compression 9.3-to-1.

Transmission: Rear-wheel drive; five-speed manual gearbox; short travel gearchange. Limited slip diff. Final drive 3.31-to-1. Top gear speed at 1000 rpm: 27.2 mph (43.8 km/h).

Suspension: Front, independent, sliding pillars and coil springs; telescopic dampers. Rear, live axle on leaf springs; lever arm dampers.

Steering: Worm and roller. Power assistance: not available.

Brakes: Discs front, drums rear, servo-assisted.

Tyres: 205/60 VR 15.   **Fuel tank:** 13.6 Imp. gall (62 litres).

Dimensions: Length 147.2 in (3740 mm), width 62 in (1575 mm), height 52 in (1320 mm), wheelbase 98 in (2490 mm).

Unladen weight: 1830 lb (830 kg).

Performance *Autocar* test: Maximum speed 123 mph (198 km/h); 0 to 60 mph (100 km/h) 6.5 sec. Fuel consumption, overall test, 20.5 mpg.

Features: Very limited vertical travel of the suspension gives extremely harsh ride and spoils roadholding; it's a car you have to fight on the rare occasions when all four wheels are in contact with the ground! But it's a real wind-in-the-hair sports car and lots of fun.

NAYLOR (GB)   MG TF 1700 Replica

Identity: Another in the series of historic cars reincarnated with modern (and far superior) running gear. Fully built-up car, with Austin Rover's O-Series engine. Chassis is exact replica of the original TF, and body is a faithful copy of the much-loved TF 1500 which ceased production 1955.

Engine: Front-mounted longitudinal four-cylinder with single belt-driven ohc. One SU carb. Bore 84.5 mm, stroke 75.8 mm; capacity 1698 cc. Power 77 bhp (57 kW) at 5180 rpm; torque 93 lb ft (129 Nm) at 3480 rpm. Compression 9.0-to-1.

Transmission: Rear-wheel drive; four-speed manual gearbox; final drive 3.64-to-1. Top gear speed at 1000 rpm: 19.3 mph (31.1 km/h).

Suspension: Front, independent, wishbones and compression strut acting on lower wishbone; telescopic coil spring and damper units. Rear, live axle with multi-link location. Direct acting telescopic coil spring and damper units.

Steering: Rack and pinion. Power assistance: not available.

Brakes: Discs front, drums rear, servo-assisted.

Tyres: 165 SR 14.   **Fuel tank:** 12.0 Imp. gall (55 litres).

Dimensions: Length 147 in (3734 mm), width 59.8 in (1519 mm), height 52.5 in (1334 mm), wheelbase 94.5 in (2400 mm).

Unladen weight: 1870 lb (848 kg).

Performance (Works): Maximum speed 94 mph (151 km/h); 0 to 60 mph (100 km/h) 11.8 sec. No fuel consumption data quoted; est. 32 mpg.

Features: Rather lively ride, but great fun to drive, looking along the narrow, pointed bonnet. Very professional construction and car has full UK type approval. Handling far better than the original.

Identity: Nissan's mid-range saloon is now in front-wheel drive form although visually there is little difference from the old model. Available as a four-door saloon or estate with 1.8- or 2.0-litre engines, and there is a performance version with 1.8-litre turbocharged engine.

Engine: Front-mounted in-line four-cylinder with single carburettor. Bore 83 mm, stroke 83.6 mm; capacity 1809 cc. Power 90 bhp (145 kW) at 5200 rpm; torque 111.8 lb ft (152 Nm) at 2800 rpm. Compression 8.0-to-1.

Transmission: Front-wheel drive; five-speed manual gearbox; four-speed automatic available with 2.0 litre model. Top gear speed at 1000 rpm: 22.7 mph (36.7 km/h).

Suspension: Front, independent, MacPherson struts and coil springs; telescopic dampers. Anti-roll bar. Rear, independent, parallel links, coil springs. Anti-roll bar.

Steering: Rack and pinion. Power assistance: not available.

Brakes: Discs front, drums rear, servo-assisted.

Tyres: 185/70 SR 14.   **Fuel tank**: 13.2 Imp. gall (60 litres).

Dimensions: Length 171.6 in (4360 mm), width 66.5 in (1690 mm), height 54.9 in (1395 mm), wheelbase 100.4 in (2550 mm).

Unladen weight: 2381 lb (1080 kg).

Performance (Works): Maximum speed 100 mph (160 km/h). Fuel consumption at constant 75 mph (120 km/h): 35.3 mpg.

Features: Straightforward 'three box' design, the Bluebird offers roomy accommodation and, in turbo form, impressive performance. The Bluebird 1.8 Turbo ZX has a claimed top speed of 121 mph. As with most Japanese models, the Bluebird has a good level of standard specification.

NISSAN (J)　　　　　　Silvia Turbo ZX

Identity: The newest, and undoubtedly the best looking, model in the Nissan UK range is the Silvia. A sports coupé with neat, restrained styling, it is available with two power unit options: a 1.8-litre four-cylinder with turbocharger or, to special order, a 2.0-litre DOHC ZX—distinguishable by a pronounced bonnet bulge.

Engine: Front-mounted in-line four-cylinder with fuel injection and turbocharger. Bore 83 mm, stroke 83.6 mm; capacity 1809 cc. Power 135 bhp (100 kW) at 6000 rpm; torque 142 lb ft (193 Nm) at 4000 rpm. Compression 8.0-to-1.

Transmission: Rear-wheel drive; five-speed manual gearbox; automatic transmission available. Top gear speed at 1000 rpm: 23.6 mph (38 km/h).

Suspension: Front, independent, struts and coil springs; telescopic dampers. Anti-roll bar. Rear, independent, semi-trailing arms and coil springs; telescopic dampers. Anti-roll bar.

Steering: Rack and pinion. Power assistance: optional.

Brakes: Ventilated front and rear, servo-assisted.

Tyres: 195/60 R 15.　　**Fuel tank:** 11.7 Imp. gall (53 litres).

Dimensions: Length 171.3 in (4351 mm), width 65.4 in (1661 mm), height 52.4 in (1330 mm), wheelbase 95.4 in (2425 mm).

Unladen weight: 2505 lb (1136 kg).

Performance (Works): Maximum speed 130 mph (209 km/h); 0 to 60 mph (100 km/h) 8.5 sec. Fuel consumption at constant 75 mph (120 km/h): 35.8 mpg.

Features: Two-door coupé body shape with lifting rear tailgate. Headlamps have 'flash only' facility, and pop-up for full use. Standard equipment includes stereo radio/cassette player and alloy wheels.

NISSAN (J)

300 ZX Turbo

Identity: The Japanese Z-car continues. This is the latest version of that famous sports car, but a far cry from the original Datsun 240Z. Completely different looks, bigger and with more power from the turbocharged V6 engine.

Engine: Front-mounted 60 deg. V6-cylinder with alloy heads, electronic injection and a Garrett turbocharger. Bore 87 mm, stroke 83 mm; capacity 2960 cc. Power 228 bhp (170 kW) at 5400 rpm; torque 242 lb ft (328 Nm) at 4400 rpm. Compression 7.4-to-1.

Transmission: Rear-wheel drive; five-speed manual gearbox. Top gear speed at 1000 rpm: 27.3 mph (43.9 km/h).

Suspension: Front, independent, struts, coil springs, telescopic dampers. Anti-roll bar. Electronically adjustable damper settings. Rear, independent, semi-trailing arms, coil springs, telescopic dampers. Anti-roll bar.

Steering: Rack and pinion. Power assistance: standard.

Brakes: Discs front and rear, servo-assisted.

Tyres: 225/55 VR 16.   **Fuel tank:** 15.8 Imp. gall (71.8 litres).

Dimensions: Length 178.5 in (4535 mm), width 67.9 in (1725 mm), height 51.6 in (1310 mm), wheelbase 91.3 in (2320 mm).

Unladen weight: 3227 lb (1464 kg).

Performance *Autocar* test: Maximum speed 137 mph (220 km/h); 0 to 60 mph (100 km/h) 7.2 sec. Fuel consumption; overall test, 21.5 mpg.

Features: Aimed very much at the American market, the 300ZX is a rather 'softer' version of the original 240Z 'muscle' car. Long wheelbase allows for 2 + 2 seating. Very high level of standard equipment.

NISSAN (J)   Prairie

Identity: Unusual design with high roof and sliding door each side, closing directly on to front-hinged door without any B-post. Very easy access, but seating capacity only for five. Top-hinged tailgate with bumper section attached allows low floor height and easy loading.

Engine: Front-mounted transverse four-cylinder with alloy head; belt-driven ohc. Nikki or Hitachi carb. Bore 76 mm, stroke 82 mm; capacity 1488 cc. Power 75 bhp (56 kW) at 5600 rpm; torque 89 lb ft (123 Nm) at 2800 rpm. Compression 9.8-to-1.

Transmission: Front-wheel drive; five-speed manual gearbox; no automatic option. Final drive 3.9-to-1. Top gear speed at 1000 rpm: 23 mph (37 km/h).

Suspension: Front, independent, MacPherson struts; coil springs and telescopic dampers. Rear, independent, trailing arms and torsion bars; telescopic dampers.

Steering: Rack and pinion. Power assistance: not available.

Brakes: Discs front, drums rear, servo-assisted.

Tyres: 165 SR 13.   **Fuel tank:** 11 Imp. gall (50 litres).

Dimensions: Length 161 in (4090 mm), width 65.2 in (1655 mm), height 63 in (1600 mm), wheelbase 98.8 in (2510 mm).

Unladen weight: 2160 lb (980 kg).

Performance *Autocar* test: Maximum speed 83 mph (133 km/h); 0 to 60 mph (100 km/h) 16.3 sec. Fuel consumption at constant 75 mph (120 km/h): 32.5 mpg; overall test, 33.1 mpg.

Features: Back seat folds flat to serve as a bed, or goes forward to provide extra luggage space. Surprisingly easy to drive due to high seating position, but not as versatile as the Toyota Model F which is, of course, considerably more expensive.

OLDSMOBILE (USA)

Calais

Identity: Newest model in the Oldsmobile line-up, the Calais was introduced for 1985. The two-door coupé is available in two engine options, four-cylinder 2.5-litre and 3-litre V6.

Engine: Front-mounted 90 degree V6-cylinder with multi-port fuel injection. Bore 96.52 mm, stroke 67.56 mm; capacity 2966 cc. Power 120 bhp (89.5 kW) at 4800 rpm; torque 150 lb ft (203 Nm) at 2600 rpm. Compression 8.45-to-1.

Transmission: Front-wheel drive; three-speed automatic gearbox, or five-speed manual standard for 2.5 litre version.

Suspension: Front, independent, MacPherson struts, coil springs; telescopic dampers. Rear, dead beam axle on semi-independent trailing arms with coil springs; telescopic dampers.

Steering: Rack and pinion. Power assistance: not available.

Brakes: Ventilated discs front, drums rear, servo-assisted.

Tyres: P205/70 R-13.   **Fuel tank:** 13.6 Imp. gall (62 litres).

Dimensions: Length 177.5 in (4508 mm), width 66.9 in (1699 mm), height 52.5 in (1333 mm), wheelbase 103.4 in (2626 mm).

Unladen weight: 2512 lb (1139 kg).

Performance (est.): Maximum speed 95 mph (152 km/h); 0 to 60 mph (100 km/h) 11.5 sec. Fuel consumption: (est.).

Features: Aimed to fit between the subcompact Firenza and mid-range Cutlass, the Calais has a good level of standard specification. Sporty bucket seats. Liquid crystal instruments.

OLDSMOBILE (USA)

Cutlass Ciera

Identity: There are no less than 15 versions of the Cutlass in the Oldsmobile model range. For 1985, the Ciera has a cleaner, more aerodynamic front end and wrap-around tail lights. It is available as a two-door coupé or sedan, in standard or Brougham trim levels.

Engine: Front-mounted V6-cylinder with multi-port Bosch fuel injection. Bore 96.52 mm, stroke 86.36 mm; capacity 3791 cc. Power 125 bhp (93.5 kW) at 4400 rpm; torque 195 lb ft (265 Nm) at 2000 rpm. Compression 8.0-to-1.

Transmission: Rear-wheel drive; four-speed automatic transmission. Top gear speed at 1000 rpm: 37.7 mph (60.7 km/h).

Suspension: Front, independent, wishbones and coil springs; telescopic dampers. Anti-roll bar. Rear, live axle on trailing arms; coil springs and telescopic dampers. Anti-roll bar.

Steering: Recirculating ball. Power assistance: standard.

Brakes: Discs front, drums rear, servo-assisted.

Tyres: 185/75-14.   **Fuel tank:** 14.0 Imp. gall (64 litres).

Dimensions: Length 188.3 in (4785 mm), width 69.4 in (1765 mm), height 54.1 in (1375 mm), wheelbase 104.9 in (2665 mm).

Unladen weight: 2711 lb (1230 kg).

Performance (Works): Maximum speed 108 mph (175 km/h). Fuel consumption: 22 mpg (est.).

Features: Detail appearance changes give the Ciera a new look for 1985; and the Ciera GT has low profile tyres and aluminium alloy wheels. The energy-absorbing rear bumper helps this Oldsmobile qualify for an insurance discount in America.

OLDSMOBILE (USA) Firenza GT Coupé

Identity: Smallest model in the Oldsmobile range is the Firenza. First introduced in 1982, it is available with 1.8-litre, 2.0-litre or—new for 1985—2.8-litre V6 engine. This is standard for the GT version.

Engine: Front-mounted 60 deg. V6-cylinder with electronic fuel injection. Bore 88.9 mm, stroke 76.2 mm; capacity 2838 cc. Power 130 bhp (97 kW) at 5400 rpm; torque 160 lb ft (217 Nm) at 2400 rpm. Compression 8.9-to-1.

Transmission: Front-wheel drive; four-speed manual gearbox; three-speed automatic available. Top gear speed at 1000 rpm: 20.9 mph (33.6 km/h).

Suspension: Front, independent, MacPherson struts and coil springs; telescopic dampers. Anti-roll bar. Rear, independent, semi-trailing arms, coil springs and telescopic dampers. Anti-roll bar.

Steering: Rack and pinion. Power assistance: optional.

Brakes: Ventilated discs front, drums rear, servo-assisted.

Tyres: 195/70 R-13. **Fuel tank:** 11.3 Imp. gall (51.5 litres).

Dimensions: Length 174.2 in (4425 mm), width 64.9 in (1650 mm), height 51.7 in (1315 mm), wheelbase 101.2 in (2570 mm).

Unladen weight: 2502 lb (1135 kg).

Performance (est.): Maximum speed 105 mph (170 km/h); 0 to 60 mph (100 km/h) 9.0 sec. Fuel consumption: 28 mpg (est.).

Features: The Coupé GT is the sporting version of the range. Models with the V6 engine can be recognized by the bulge in the bonnet and the slightly larger grille area to aid cooling.

OLDSMOBILE (USA)   Toronado Caliente

Identity: Top of the Oldsmobile range is the Toronado, of which the luxury version is the Caliente. Two-door coupé body only. For 1985 the 5-litre V8 engine is standard; a 5.7-litre diesel engine remains available as an option.

Engine: Front-mounted, 90 deg. V8-cylinder with single Rochester carburettor. Bore 96.5 mm, stroke 85.9 mm; capacity 5033 cc. Power 140 bhp (104 kW) at 3600 rpm; torque 240 lb ft (326 Nm) at 1600 rpm. Compression 8.0-to-1.

Transmission: Front-wheel drive; three-speed Hydra-Matic automatic with overdrive. No manual option. Top gear speed at 1000 rpm: 40 mph (64 km/h).

Suspension: Front, independent, wishbones and longitudinal torsion bars; telescopic dampers. Anti-roll bar. Rear, independent, semi-trailing arms and coil springs; telescopic dampers. Pneumatic self-levelling. Anti-roll bar.

Steering: Recirculating ball. Power assistance: standard.

Brakes: Ventilated discs front, drums rear, servo-assisted.

Tyres: 205/75 R 15.   **Fuel tank:** 17.6 Imp. gall (80 litres).

Dimensions: Length 206 in (5232 mm), width 71.4 in (1814 mm), height 55.2 in (1400 mm), wheelbase 114 in (2896 mm).

Unladen weight: 3887 lb (1763 kg).

Performance (est.): Maximum speed 110 mph (177 km/h). Fuel consumption: 20 mph (est.).

Features: Personal luxury coupé, with padded landau roof covering; stainless steel crown moulding. Bright body mouldings. Standard interior includes leather trim and electronic instrument panel.

Identity: New engines and other improvements transformed the Opel Manta in 1982, and at the 1983 Geneva Show a fuel injection version was launched (on British market July). 'Manta GTE' lettered on body sides, and spoiler at base of rear window. Distinctive alloy wheels finished in silver. Two-door coupé or hatchback.

Engine: Front-mounted longitudinal four-cylinder with chain-driven camshaft in head; hydraulic tappets. Bosch LE Jetronic fuel injection. Bore 95 mm, stroke 70 mm; capacity 1979 cc. Power 110 bhp (82 kW) at 5400 rpm; torque 120 lb ft (165 Nm) at 3400 rpm. Compression 9.4-to-1.

Transmission: Rear-wheel drive; five-speed manual gearbox; GM three-speed automatic transmission available. Top gear speed at 1000 rpm: 24.4 mph (39.3 km/h).

Suspension: Front, independent, wishbones and coil springs; anti-dive effect. Bilstein telescopic dampers. Anti-roll bar. Rear, live axle on trailing arms with lateral track rod; coil springs and Bilstein dampers.

Steering: Rack and pinion. Power assistance: not available.

Brakes: Discs front, drums rear, servo-assisted.

Tyres: 195/60 HR 14.   **Fuel tank**: 11 Imp. gall (50 litres).

Dimensions: Length 172.6 in (4384 mm), width 66.4 in (1686 mm), height 57.8 in (1315 mm), wheelbase 99 in (2520 mm).

Unladen weight: 2403 lb (1090 kg).

Performance *Autocar* test: Maximum speed 120 mph (193 km/h); 0 to 60 mph (100 km/h) 10.0 sec. Fuel consumption at constant 75 mph (120 km/h): 37.1 mpg; overall test, 29.1 mpg.

Features: Sporty and responsive car to drive; suspension a little firm, but cornering is excellent. Generous equipment.

OPEL (D)   Monza GSE

Identity: Very attractive high performance GT. Spoiler at base of hatchback window identifies revised version, launched Frankfurt 1983. Only one model in UK, with 3-litre engine; but some markets have 2-litre and 2.5-litre Monzas.

Engine: Front-mounted longitudinal six-cylinder with chain-driven camshaft in head; hydraulic tappets. Bosch L-Jetronic fuel injection. Bore 95 mm, stroke 68.9 mm; capacity 2968 cc. Power 177 bhp (132 kW) at 5800 rpm; torque 179 lb ft (248 Nm) at 4800 rpm. Compression 9.4-to-1.

Transmission: Rear-wheel drive; five-speed manual gearbox; three-speed automatic optional at no extra cost. Top gear speed at 1000 rpm: 23.5 mph (37.8 km/h).

Suspension: Front, independent, MacPherson struts and coil springs; telescopic dampers. Anti-roll bar. Rear, independent, semi-trailing arms and mini-block coil springs; telescopic dampers. Anti-roll bar.

Steering: Recirculating ball. Power assistance: standard.

Brakes: Vented discs front, solid discs rear, servo-assisted.

Tyres: 205/60 VR 15.   **Fuel tank:** 15.4 Imp. gall (70 litres).

Dimensions: Length 185.8 in (4720 mm), width 67.8 in (1722 mm), height 54.3 in (1380 mm), wheelbase 105 in (2668 mm).

Unladen weight: 3268 lb (1484 kg).

Performance *Autocar* test: Maximum speed 132 mph (212 km/h); 0 to 60 mph (100 km/h) 8.7 sec. Fuel consumption at constant 75 mph (120 km/h): 30.1 mpg; overall test, 20.5 mpg.

Features: Extremely good handling, comfortable ride and effortless high performance combine to make this a most likeable car. Sports seats. Lavish equipment including digital and graphical instrumentation.

PANTHER (GB)

Kallista 2.8i

Identity: Production concentrated at first on the 1.6-litre version of this most beautifully finished and traditional-style two-seater; but as promised at the launch (Birmingham 1982), the Ford 2.8 injection engine became available 1984. Aluminium bodywork. Folding hood, and winding side windows.

Engine: Front-mounted longitudinal V6-cylinder with pushrod ohv. Cast iron heads and block. Bosch K-Jetronic fuel injection; carburettor V6 also available. Bore 93 mm, stroke 68 mm; capacity 2792 cc. Power 148 bhp (110 kW) at 5700 rpm; torque 156 lb ft (216 Nm) at 4000 rpm. Compression 9.2-to-1.

Transmission: Rear-wheel drive; five-speed manual gearbox; three-speed automatic transmission optional. Top gear speed at 1000 rpm: 26.7 mph (43 km/h).

Suspension: Front, independent, wishbones and coil springs; telescopic dampers. Rear, live axle on trailing links, with Panhard rod and coil springs; telescopic dampers.

Steering: Rack and pinion. Power assistance: not available.

Brakes: Discs front, drums rear, servo-assisted.

Tyres: 185/70 HR 13.   **Fuel tank:** 10 Imp. gall (45.5 litres).

Dimensions: Length 153.7 in (3905 mm), width 67.4 in (1712 mm), height 49 in (1245 mm), wheelbase 100.3 in (2549 mm).

Unladen weight: 2070 lb (940 kg).

Performance *Autocar* test: Maximum speed 109 mph (175 km/h); 0 to 60 mph (100 km/h) 7.7 sec. Fuel consumption, overall test, 24.4 mpg.

Features: Exciting car to drive, looking down on long, tapering bonnet and chromed headlamps. Quite good ride and steering; handling fair.

PEUGEOT (F)

205 GTI

Identity: Top of the successful 205 range is the attractive GTI. Good looks and sparkling performance combine to make this a very desirable member of the 'hot hatchback' club. Available only in three-door form.

Engine: Front-mounted transverse, four-cylinder with Bosch L-Jetronic fuel injection. Bore 83 mm, stroke 73 mm; capacity 1580 cc. Power 105 bhp (77 kW) at 6250 rpm; torque 99 lb ft (134 Nm) at 4000 rpm. Compression 10.2-to-1.

Transmission: Front-wheel drive; five-speed manual gearbox. Top gear speed at 1000 rpm: 18.7 mph (30 km/h).

Suspension: Front, independent, MacPherson struts, lower wishbones, coil springs, telescopic dampers. Anti-roll bar. Rear, independent, trailing arms transverse torsion bars, telescopic dampers. Anti-roll bar.

Steering: Rack and pinion. Power assistance: not available.

Brakes: Ventilated discs front, drums rear, servo-assisted.

Tyres: 185/60 R-14.   **Fuel tank:** 11 Imp. gall (50 litres).

Dimensions: Length 145.9 in (3705 mm), width 61.9 in (1572 mm), height 53.3 in (1355 mm), wheelbase 95.3 in (2420 mm).

Unladen weight: 2004 lb (909 kg).

Performance *Autocar* test: Maximum speed 116 mph (187 km/h); 0 to 60 mph (100 km/h) 8.6 sec. Fuel consumption; overall test, 29.5 mpg.

Features: Hot hatchbacks are latterday sports cars, and the 205 GTI is a prime example. Good performance and handling characteristics make it tremendous fun to drive.

PEUGEOT (F)

Identity: Peugeot's medium-sized 305 family saloon and estate car ranges date back to 1977, but all substantially updated in 1982. Available with petrol and diesel engines, and the sporting version, the GT model, has the 'co-op' engine also used in the Citroen BX. New fast GTX and 305 Automatic launched Birmingham 1984.

Engine: Front-mounted transverse four-cylinder with belt driven ohc. Alloy head and block; cast iron liners. Bore 83 mm, stroke 88 mm; capacity 1905 cc. Power 105 bhp (78 kW) at 5600 rpm; torque 119 lb ft (165 Nm) at 3000 rpm. Compression 9.3-to-1.

Transmission: Front-wheel drive; five-speed manual gearbox; no automatic option. Top gear speed at 1000 rpm: 20.5 mph (33.0 km/h).

Suspension: Front, independent, MacPherson struts, coil springs and telescopic dampers. Anti-roll bar. Rear, independent trailing arms, coil springs and telescopic dampers. Anti-roll bar.

Steering: Rack and pinion. Power assistance: not available.

Brakes: Discs front, drums rear, servo-assisted.

Tyres: 185/60 HR-14.   **Fuel tank:** 11.6 Imp. gall (52.7 litres).

Dimensions: Length 167.8 in (4262 mm), width 64.4 in (1636 mm), height 55.5 in (1410 mm), wheelbase 103.2 in (2620 mm).

Unladen weight: 2170 lb (984 kg).

Performance (Works): Maximum speed 112 mph (180 km/h); 0 to 60 mph (100 km/h) 10.8 sec. Fuel consumption at constant 75 mph (120 km/h): 37.2 mph.

Features: Very easy to drive, and with Peugeot's characteristically comfortable ride, the 305 range has lasted the test of time well. The GTX form has subtle sporting aspirations, and is visually distinguished by the boot lid spoiler and body side stripes.

PEUGEOT (F)   505 GL Diesel Estate car

Identity: Last year we featured the Peugeot 505 petrol estate car, but having made a long Continental journey in 1984 using a diesel version, I felt this model was certainly worthy of inclusion in the 1985 edition. Very competent, roomy, and extremely comfortable load carrier with the advantage of diesel economy, yet still quite good performance.

Engine: Front-mounted longitudinal four-cylinder with pushrod ohv. Alloy head, cast iron cylinder block. Bore 94 mm, stroke 90 mm; capacity 2498 cc. Power 76 bhp (57 kW) at 4500 rpm; torque 111 lb ft (153 Nm) at 2000 rpm. Compression 23.0-to-1.

Transmission: Rear-wheel drive; five-speed manual gearbox; no automatic transmission option for diesel models. Top gear speed at 1000 rpm: 24.2 mph (39 km/h).

Suspension: Front, independent, MacPherson struts and coil springs; telescopic dampers. Anti-roll bar. Rear, live axle on trailing arms; coil springs and telescopic dampers. Anti-roll bar.

Steering: Rack and pinion. Power assistance: standard.

Brakes: Discs front, drums rear, servo-assisted.

Tyres: 185 SR 14.   **Fuel tank:** 12.3 Imp. gall (56 litres).

Dimensions: Length 192 in (4898 mm), width 68 in (1730 mm), height 60.6 in (1540 mm), wheelbase 114.2 in (2900 mm).

Unladen weight: 3054 lb (1385 kg).

Performance (Works): Maximum speed 91 mph (146 km/h); 0 to 60 mph (100 km/h) 19.5 sec. Fuel consumption at constant 75 mph (120 km/h): 31.4 mpg.

Features: Deep load compartment and curved rear door makes generous load space available. Very comfortable seats and ride. Neatly finished and solidly built. Not too noisy in spite of diesel engine.

PININFARINA (I)   Spidereuropa Volumex

Identity: Derived from former Fiat 124, this attractive little four-seater convertible is built by Pininfarina, and supercharged version was launched mid-1983 using Lancia Trevi Volumex engine. Improvements Paris 1984 included rack and pinion steering. Supercharged version identified by Volumex name on bonnet.

Engine: Front-mounted longitudinal four-cylinder with belt-driven twin ohc. Separate belt drives the supercharger. Electronic fuel injection and ignition. Bore 84 mm, stroke 90 mm; capacity 1995 cc. Power 135 bhp (99 kW) at 5500 rpm; torque 149 lb ft (206 Nm) at 3000 rpm. Compression 7.5-to-1.

Transmission: Rear-wheel drive; five-speed manual gearbox; no automatic option. Top gear speed at 1000 rpm: 22.9 mph (36.9 km/h).

Suspension: Front, independent, wishbones and triangular helix-shaped coil springs; telescopic dampers. Anti-roll bar. Rear, independent, semi-trailing arms with helical coil springs and Bilstein dampers.

Steering: Rack and pinion. Power assistance: not available.

Brakes: Vented discs front, solid discs rear, servo-assisted.

Tyres: 185/60 SR 14 P7.   **Fuel tank:** 9.9 Imp. gall (45 litres).

Dimensions: Length 163 in (4140 mm), width 100 in (1615 mm), height 49 in (1250 mm), wheelbase 89.9 in (2280 mm).

Unladen weight: 2315 lb (1050 kg).

Performance (Works): Maximum speed 118 mph (190 km/h); 0 to 60 mph (100 km/h) 9 sec. Fuel consumption at constant 75 mph (120 km/h): 28.8 mpg.

Features: Improvements for 1985 include larger brake discs, new alloy wheels and improved water cooling.

PLYMOUTH (USA)   Gran Fury

Identity: This is the large model in the Plymouth range, with squared-up four-door saloon body. Slab front houses four headlamps. Flush wheel trims. Choice of six-cylinder or V8 engine.

Engine: Front-mounted longitudinal V8-cylinder with hydraulic tappets, and central chain-driven camshaft. Carter twin-choke carb. Bore 99.3mm, stroke 84.1 mm; capacity 5210 cc. Power 130 bhp (97 kW) at 4000 rpm; torque 230 lb ft (319 Nm) at 1600 rpm. Compression 8.5-to-1.

Transmission: Rear-wheel drive; Chrysler Torqueflite three-speed automatic transmission standard (no manual transmission option). Top gear speed at 1000 rpm: 29.0 mph (46.8 km/h).

Suspension: Front, independent, wishbones and transverse torsion bars; telescopic dampers. Anti-roll bar. Rear, live axle on semi-elliptic leaf springs; telescopic dampers. Anti-roll bar optional.

Steering: Recirculating ball. Power assistance: standard.

Brakes: Vented discs front; drums rear, servo-assisted.

Tyres: 205/75 R 15.   **Fuel tank:** 15 Imp. gall (68 litres).

Dimensions: Length 205.7 in (5225 mm), width 74 in (1885 mm), height 55.3 in (1405 mm), wheelbase 1128 in (2865 mm).

Unladen weight: 3560 lb (1615kg).

Performance (Works): Maximum speed 106 mph (170 km/h). Fuel consumption, overall (test), 17 mpg.

Features: Opulent and spacious model of the Plymouth range, the Gran Fury has much in common with the Chrysler Fifth Avenue. Long tail gives generous luggage space, and interior offers lavish seating for five. Bright trims to wheel housings. Frontal styling continues centre grille out to front corners of car.

Identity: The Pontiac Fiero is the first new mass production, two-seater American sports car since the Thunderbird in 1955. Mid-engined, the Fiero has a basic steel space frame carrying plastic body panels. Engine is a 2.5-litre in-line four-cylinder; new for 1985 is a 2.8-litre V6 fuel injection unit.

Engine: Mid-mounted, in-line four-cylinder with overhead valves, cast iron head and block. Bore 101.6 mm, stroke 76.2 mm; capacity 2471 cc. Power 92 bhp (68 kW) at 4000 rpm; torque 134 lb ft (182 Nm) at 2800 rpm. Compression 9-to-1.

Transmission: Rear-wheel drive; five-speed manual gearbox. Top gear speed at 1000 rpm: 26.4 mph (42.5 km/h).

Suspension: Front, independent, unequal length upper and lower control arms and coil springs; telescopic dampers. Anti-roll bar. Rear, independent, MacPherson struts, coil springs; telescopic dampers.

Steering: Rack and pinion. Power assistance: not available.

Brakes: Discs front, drums rear, servo-assisted.

Tyres: 215/60 R-13.   **Fuel tank:** 8.5 Imp. gall (38.5 litres).

Dimensions: Length 160.7 in (4081 mm), width 68.9 in (1750 mm), height 46.9 in (1191 mm), wheelbase 93.4 in (2372 mm).

Unladen weight: 2458 lb (1115 kg).

Performance (Works): Maximum speed 111 mph (180 km/h); 0 to 60 mph (100 km/h) 11.5 sec. Fuel consumption: 31 mpg (est.).

Features: Stylish two-seater sports that has broken the Detroit mould in its use of plastics and position of engine. Slightly lack-lustre performance in four-cylinder form, improved if V6 engine is chosen instead.

PONTIAC (USA)   Sunbird LE convertible

Identity: Adapted from the General Motors European model range, as the Opel Manta, the Sunbird (the 1984 designation 2000 has been dropped) is available with 1.8-litre engines with or without turbocharger. Body styles are notchback, coupé or convertible.

Engine: Front-mounted transverse four-cylinder with Garrett turbocharger. Alloy head. Belt driven ohc. Bosch L-Jetronic injection. Bore 84.8 mm, stroke 79.5 mm; capacity 1796 cc. Power 150 bhp (112 kW) at 5600 rpm; torque 150 lb ft (207 Nm) at 2800 rpm. Compression 8.0-to-1.

Transmission: Front-wheel drive; five-speed manual gearbox; three-speed automatic transmission available. Top gear speed at 1000 rpm: 22.7 mph (36.6 km/h).

Suspension: Front, independent, MacPherson struts and coil springs; telescopic dampers. Anti-roll bar. Rear, independent, trailing arms, coil springs; telescopic dampers. Anti-roll bar.

Steering: Rack and pinion. Power assistance: optional.

Brakes: Discs front, drums rear, servo-assisted.

Tyres: 205/60 R-14.   **Fuel tank:** 11.2 Imp. gall (51 litres).

Dimensions: Length 175.4 in (4455 mm), width 65.7 in (1670 mm), height 53.9 in (1370 mm), wheelbase 101.2 in (2570 mm).

Unladen weight: 2512 lb (1140 kg).

Performance (Works): Maximum speed 118 mph (190 km/h); 0 to 60 mph (100 km/h) 10.0 sec. Fuel consumption: 32.0 mpg (est.).

Features: Ducting on bonnet for turbo models denotes 1985 versions. Large choice of optional equipment. Simple to operate manual hood for convertible.

Identity: American muscle car, the Pontiac Firebird is available with a wide choice of power units; four-cylinder 2.5-litre, V6 2.8-litre or V8 5-litre. Most powerful version is the Firebird Trans Am (detailed here).

Engine: Front-mounted V8-cylinder with Rochester Quadrajet carburettor. Bore 94.89 mm, stroke 88.39 mm; capacity 5001 cc. Power 193 bhp (142 kW) at 4800 rpm; torque 240 lb ft (326 Nm) at 3200 rpm. Compression 9.5-to-1.

Transmission: Rear-wheel drive; five-speed manual gearbox; three-speed automatic available only with 2.5-litre engine. Top gear speed at 1000 rpm: 27.5 mph (44.3 km/h).

Suspension: Front, independent, wishbones, lower trailing links, and coil springs; telescopic dampers. Anti-roll bar. Rear, live axle, semi-elliptic leaf springs; telescopic dampers. Anti-roll bar.

Steering: Rack and pinion.

Brakes: Ventilated discs front, drums rear, servo-assisted.

Tyres: 215/65 R-15.   **Fuel tank:** 13.4 Imp. gall (61 litres).

Dimensions: Length 189.9 in (4825 mm), width 72.4 in (1840 mm), height 49.6 in (1260 mm), wheelbase 109.0 in (2565 mm).

Unladen weight: 3185 lb (1445 kg).

Performance (est.): Maximum speed 125 mph (200 km/h). Fuel consumption: 18 mph (est.).

Features: Well-established American sports car. Trans Am has front and rear spoilers and side skirt aerodynamic aids. Air conditioning is available as an option.

Identity: At one time it was thought that 911 production would end, but now it seems set to continue indefinitely. Engine capacity increased to 3.2 litres Frankfurt 1983, with new gearbox ratios and better brakes, designated Carrera. Coupé, Targa, and the Cabriolet, are offered.

Engine: Rear-mounted horizontally opposed six-cylinder with air cooling. Chain-driven single ohc on each bank. Bosch Motronics injection and ignition. Bore 95 mm, stroke 74.4 mm; capacity 3164 cc. Power 228 bhp (170 kW) at 5900 rpm; torque 205 lb ft (284 Nm) at 4800 rpm. Compression 10.3-to-1.

Transmission: Rear-wheel drive; five-speed manual gearbox; gearbox in unit with engine at rear. No automatic option. Top gear speed at 1000 rpm: 23.6 mph (38.0 km/h).

Suspension: Front, independent, MacPherson struts and torsion bars; telescopic dampers. Anti-roll bar. Rear, independent, semi-trailing arms and torsion bars. Anti-roll bar.

Steering: Rack and pinion. Power assistance: not available.

Brakes: Vented discs front and rear, servo-assisted.

Tyres: 185/70 VR 15 front; 215/60 VR 15 rear. **Fuel tank:** 17.6 Imp. gall (80 litres).

Dimensions: Length 168.9 in (4291 mm), width 65 in (1652 mm), height 52 in (1320 mm), wheelbase 89.5 in (2273 mm).

Unladen weight: 2558 lb (1160 kg).

Performance *Autocar* test: Maximum speed 150 mph (242 km/h); 0 to 60 mph (100 km/h) 5.4 sec. Fuel consumption at constant 75 mph (120 km/h): 31.4 mpg; overall test, 22.2 mpg.

Features: Very noisy at speed, especially when open, but shatteringly fast, neat hood, with detachable levers for screen rail fastenings. Expensive.

Identity: New in Germany in mid-1981, high-performance derivative of 924, with Porsche's own new 2½-litre four-cylinder engine. Body basically the same, but note the enlarged wheel arches and deep front spoiler. Power steering standard from 1984.

Engine: Front-mounted four-cylinder with alloy block and head, linerless block. Breakerless ignition; Bosch L Jetronic fuel injection. Bore 100 mm, stroke 78.9 mm; capacity 2479 cc. Power 161 bhp (120 kW) at 5800 rpm; torque 148 lb ft (205 Nm) at 3000 rpm. Compression 10.6-to-1.

Transmission: Rear-wheel drive; five-speed manual gearbox; three-speed automatic transmission optional. Top gear speed at 1000 rpm: 22.8 mph (36.6 km/h).

Suspension: Front, independent, MacPherson struts; coil springs and telescopic dampers. Anti-roll bar. Rear, independent, semi-trailing arms and torsion bars; telescopic dampers. Anti-roll bar.

Steering: Rack and pinion. Power assistance: standard.

Brakes: Vented discs front and rear, servo-assisted.

Tyres: 215/60 VR 15.   **Fuel tank:** 14.5 Imp. gall (66 litres).

Dimensions: Length 165.3 in (4200 mm), width 68.3 in (1735 mm), height 50 in (1275 mm), wheelbase 94.5 in (2400 mm).

Unladen weight: 2632 lb (1195 kg).

Performance *Autocar* test: Maximum speed 137 mph (220 km/h); 0 to 60 mph (100 km/h) 7.4 sec. Fuel consumption at constant 75 mph (120 km/h): 30.1 mpg; overall test, 26.2 mpg.

Features: As for 924, gearbox is at rear in transaxle, with torque tube for prop shaft of small diameter. Four high-back seats, minimal rear legroom; opening rear window. Remote electric release for rear hatch. Removable roof panel with electric tilt available.

Identity: Transaxle arrangement (gearbox with final drive at the rear) aids excellent roadholding. 1985 model offers marginal power increase for engine with four-speed automatic gearbox now available. Anti-lock brakes also fitted as standard.

Engine: Front-mounted V8-cylinder with all-alloy construction. Single belt-driven ohc on each bank. Hydraulic tappets. Bore 97 mm, stroke 78.9 mm; capacity 4664 cc. Power 310 bhp (230 kW) at 5900 rpm; torque 294 lb ft (399 Nm) at 4500 rpm. Compression 10.4-to-1.

Transmission: Rear-wheel drive; five-speed manual gearbox; four-speed automatic optional. Top gear speed at 1000 rpm: 25.6 mph (41.2 km/h).

Suspension: Front, independent, wishbones, coaxial coil springs and telescopic dampers. Anti-roll bar. Rear, independent, semi-trailing arms with self-compensating wheel alignment control in severe cornering (Weissach axle), coil springs and telescopic dampers. Anti-roll bar.

Steering: Rack and pinion. Power assistance: standard.

Brakes: Ventilated discs front and rear, servo-assisted.

Tyres: 225/50 VR 16.   **Fuel tank:** 18.9 Imp. gall (86 litres).

Dimensions: Length 175.1 in (4448 mm), width 72.3 in (1836 mm), height 51.7 in (1313 mm), wheelbase 98.4 in (2499 mm).

Unladen weight: 3197 lb (1450 kg).

Performance *Autocar* test: Maximum speed 158 mph (254 km/h); 0 to 60 mph (100 km/h) 6.2 sec. Fuel consumption; overall test, 16.6 mpg.

Features: High standard of luxury specification to match the performance and price. Diminutive 2 + 2 rear seats tip forward to increase load area. Inclined headlamps swing forward for use.

Identity: New sports car aimed at the gap in the market left by demise of the MG and Triumph sporting models, and very economically priced. Launched Birmingham, 1984; on market early 1985. Powered by either Ford CVH 1300 or 1600 engines.

Engine: Front-mounted four-cylinder with twin-choke downdraught Weber carburettor. Ohc, hydraulic tappets. Bore 79.96 mm, stroke 79.92 mm; capacity 1596 cc. Power 96 bhp (71.5 kW) at 6000 rpm; torque 98 lb ft (133 Nm) at 4000 rpm. Compression 9.5-to-1.

Transmission: Rear-wheel drive; five-speed manual gearbox. Four-speed for 1300-engined version. Top gear speed at 1000 rpm (five-speed gearbox): 20.4 mph (32.8 km/h).

Suspension: Front, independent, wishbones, coil springs and telescopic dampers. Separate anti-roll bar. Rear, independent semi-trailing arms, coil springs, telescopic dampers. Anti-roll bar.

Steering: Rack and pinion. Power assistance: not available.

Brakes: Disc front, drums rear, servo-assisted.

Tyres: 185/60 SR-14.   **Fuel tank:** 10 Imp. gall (45.4 litres).

Dimensions: Length 153 in (3886 mm), width 62.3 in (1582 mm), height 48.8 in (1240 mm), wheelbase 84 in (2133 mm).

Unladen weight: 1850 lb (839 kg).

Performance (Works, for 1600): Maximum speed 110 mph (177 km/h); 0 to 60 mph (100 km/h) 9.6 sec. Fuel consumption at constant 75 mph (120 km/h): 35.9 mpg.

Features: Interesting new sports car. Space frame 'backbone' chassis has easily removable, damage-resistant polyurethane and polyester plastic outer body panels. Removeable hard top available. Headlamps tip forward to vertical for use, as Porsche 928.

RELIANT (GB) Scimitar GTC

Identity: Alongside the new small sports car, SS-1, the GTE and GTC (convertible) continue for 1985. Four-seater with glass fibre body on galvanized steel chassis. Hood folds down into a well behind back seat, leaving fixed roll bar in position. Ford Cologne 2.8-litre engine.

Engine: Front-mounted V6-cylinder with pushrod ohv. Weber carb. Bore 93 mm, stroke 68.5 mm; capacity 2792 cc. Power 135 bhp (101 kW) at 5200 rpm; torque 159 lb ft (220 Nm) at 3000 rpm. Compression 9.2-to-1.

Transmission: Rear-wheel drive; four-speed manual gearbox plus overdrive operating on third and fourth. Three-speed automatic optional. Top gear speed at 1000 rpm: 26.7 mph (43.0 km/h).

Suspension: Front, independent, wishbones and coil springs; telescopic dampers. Anti-roll bar. Rear, live axle on trailing arms with Watts linkage; coil springs and telescopic dampers.

Steering: Rack and pinion. Power assistance: optional.

Brakes: Discs front, drums rear, servo-assisted.

Tyres: 185 HR 14.   **Fuel tank:** 20 Imp. gall (91 litres).

Dimensions: Length 174.5 in (4432 mm), width 67.8 in (1720 mm), height 52 in (1321 mm), wheelbase 103.8 in (2637 mm).

Unladen weight: 2790 lb (1266 kg).

Performance: Maximum speed 119 mph (192 km/h); 0 to 60 mph (100 km/h) 10.0 sec. Fuel consumption at constant 75 mph (120 km/h): 29.4 mpg.

Features: Overdrive standard unless automatic transmission is specified. Long-legged fast cruising car with the appeal of a fully convertible four-seater. Fixed roll bar remains in place when hood is down.

RENAULT (F)   5 GTL

Identity: The original Renault 5 was introduced as far back as 1972. The new version, launched September 1984, looks similar to the old but underneath there are big changes—mainly the position of the engine—now transverse; previously it was in-line. The front suspension is also new. There are eleven models and three engine variants.

Engine: Front-mounted transverse, four-cylinder with cast iron block, alloy head. Bore 76 mm, stroke 77 mm; capacity 1397 cc. Power 60 bhp (45 kW) at 5250 rpm; torque 77 lb ft (104 Nm) at 2500 rpm. Compression 9.25-to-1.

Transmission: Front-wheel drive; five-speed manual gearbox. Top gear speed at 1000 rpm: 23.8 mph (38.3 km/h).

Suspension: Front, independent, MacPherson struts, lower wishbones and coil springs; telescopic dampers. Rear, independent, trailing arms, transverse torsion bar springing using co-axial units; telescopic dampers. Anti-roll bar.

Steering: Rack and pinion.

Brakes: Discs front, drums rear, servo-assisted.

Tyres: 155/70-13.   **Fuel tank:** 9.5 Imp. gall (43 litres).

Dimensions: Length 141.4 in (3591 mm), width 62.2 in (1585 mm), height 54.7 in (1389 mm), wheelbase 94.8 in (2407 mm).

Unladen weight: 1609 lb (730 kg).

Performance (Works): Maximum speed 98 mph (157 km/h); 0 to 60 mph (100 km/h) 14.0 sec. Fuel consumption at constant 75 mph (120 km/h): 45.6 mpg; overall test, 48.5 mpg.

Features: Nicknamed the 'Superfive', there are seven versions for the UK. Also the GT Turbo is claimed to have a top speed of 124 mph for competition.

145

Identity: The 11 is the hatchback version of the Renault 9 and it was given the turbocharger treatment in early 1984. Available in three-door hatchback form, the Garrett AiResearch Turbocharger gives the car 116 mph performance.

Engine: Front-mounted transverse four-cylinder with side-mounted camshaft, alloy head, Garrett turbocharger. Bore 76 mm, stroke 77 mm; capacity 1397 cc. Power 105 bhp (77 kW) at 5500 rpm; torque 119 lb ft (162 Nm) at 2500 rpm. Compression 8.05-to-1.

Transmission: Front-wheel drive; five-speed manual gearbox with close ratios. Top gear speed at 1000 rpm: 21.3 mph (34.2 km/h).

Suspension: Front, independent, MacPherson struts, coil springs; telescopic dampers. Anti-roll bar. Rear, independent, trailing arms, torsion bars; telescopic dampers. Anti-roll bar.

Steering: Rack and pinion. Power assistance: not available.

Brakes: Ventilated discs front, drums rear, servo-assisted.

Tyres: 175/65 HR 14.   **Fuel tank:** 10.3 Imp. gall (46.8 litres).

Dimensions: Length 156.4 in (3973 mm), width 64.2 in (1630 mm), height 55.5 in (1410 mm), wheelbase 97.8 in (2483 mm).

Unladen weight: 2017 lb (915 kg).

Performance *Autocar* test: Maximum speed 116 mph (187 km/h); 0 to 60 mph (100 km/h) 8.7 sec. Fuel consumption at constant 75 mph (120 km/h): 35.8 mpg; overall test, 27.0 mpg.

Features: The Turbo is easily recognizable by its front and rear spoilers and light alloy wheels. The model also has a high level of standard specification including Renault's excellent 'remote' central door locking, electric windows and leather covered sports steering wheel.

RENAULT (F)   **Fuego GTX Turbo**

Identity: One of the most pleasing GT cars I drove during 1984 was the Fuego Turbo. Launched Frankfurt 1983. Turbo version now automatically gets top-level GTX trim; GTS version with non-turbo 1647 cc engine continues, but former 1995 cc version discontinued.

Engine: Front-mounted longitudinal four-cylinder with light alloy block and head. Wet cylinder liners. Pushrod ohv and inclined valves. Garrett T3 turbocharger. Bore 77 mm, stroke 84 mm; capacity 1565 cc. Power 130 bhp (97 kW) at 5500 rpm; torque 145 lb ft (200 Nm) at 3000 rpm. Compression 8.0-to-1.

Transmission: Front-wheel drive; five-speed manual gearbox; no automatic option. Final drive 3.78-to-1. Top gear speed at 1000 rpm: 24.3 mph (39 km/h).

Suspension: Front, independent, wishbones and coil springs; telescopic dampers. Anti-roll bar. Rear, dead beam axle on longitudinal links and central triangular link, with coil springs; telescopic dampers. Anti-roll bar.

Steering: Rack and pinion. Power assistance: standard.

Brakes: Vented discs front, solid discs rear, servo-assisted.

Tyres: 185/65 HR 14.   **Fuel tank:** 12.5 Imp. gall (57 litres).

Dimensions: Length 172.5 in (4384 mm), width 66.6 in (1692 mm), height 52.6 in (1336 mm), wheelbase 96 in (2440 mm).

Unladen weight: 2303 lb (1045 kg).

Performance *Autocar* test: Maximum speed 118 mph (190 km/h); 0 to 60 mph (100 km/h) 9.3 sec. Fuel consumption at constant 75 mph (120 km/h): 36.7 mpg; overall test, 25.0 mpg.

Features: Well equipped and very comfortable sporting GT with on-board computer for average speed, fuel consumption and other journey calculations.

Identity: Launched in November 1983, the new 25 range was included in V6 form in the 1984 edition; this year we feature the very impressive GTX with four-cylinder injection engine. The 25 was worthy winner of the Guild of Motoring Writers Top Car Award 1985.

Engine: Front-mounted longitudinal four-cylinder with alloy construction, wet liners. Belt-driven ohc. Renault multi-point fuel injection. Bore 88 mm, stroke 89 mm; capacity 2165 cc. Power 123 bhp (92 kW) at 5250 rpm; torque 134 lb ft (185 Nm) at 2750 rpm. Compression 9.9-to-1.

Transmission: Front-wheel drive; five-speed manual gearbox; three-speed automatic optional. Final drive 3.89-to-1 (automatic 3.56). Top gear speed at 1000 rpm: 22.1 mph (35.6 km/h).

Suspension: Front, independent, wishbones and coil springs; telescopic dampers. Anti-roll bar. Rear, independent, MacPherson struts and varying rate coil springs; telescopic dampers. Anti-roll bar.

Steering: Rack and pinion. Power assistance: standard.

Brakes: Vented discs front, drums rear, servo-assisted.

Tyres: 165/80 R 14.   **Fuel tank:** 15.8 Imp. gall (72 litres).

Dimensions: Length 181.9 in (4620 mm), width 69.7 in (1770 mm), height 55 in (1400 mm), wheelbase 107.2 in (2723 mm).

Unladen weight: 2646 lb (1200 kg).

Performance (Works): Maximum speed 121 mph (195 km/h); 0 to 60 mph (100 km/h) 10.3 sec. Fuel consumption at constant 75 mph (120 km/h): 35.8 mpg.

Features: Very comfortable and roomy car, with four-door body which looks like a saloon but actually has opening rear hatch as well. Versatile rear seating arrangement. Generous standard equipment in GTX spec. includes magnificent built-in radio with remote control and amplifier.

ROLLS-ROYCE (GB)   Corniche convertible

Identity: Although similar to the now-discontinued Silver Shadow, the Corniche has all the suspension revisions of the later Spirit, and was in fact up-dated in this respect before Silver Spirit was introduced. Two-door four-seater convertible with electrically-operated hood.

Engine: Front-mounted V8-cylinder with alloy block and heads hydraulic tappets. Single Solex carb. Bore, 104.1 mm, stroke 99.1 mm; capacity 6750 cc. Power and torque—no data disclosed by Rolls-Royce. Compression 9.0-to-1.

Transmission: Rear-wheel drive; GM 400 automatic transmission standard with Rolls-Royce electric selector on steering column. Top gear speed at 1000 rpm: 26.3 mph (42.3 km/h).

Suspension: Front, independent, wishbones and coil springs; telescopic dampers. Anti-roll bar. Rear, independent, trailing arms, coil springs, and hydro-pneumatic auxiliary springs, with self-levelling provision. Telescopic dampers; anti-roll bar.

Steering: Rack and pinion. Power assistance: standard.

Brakes: Vented discs front, solid discs rear, servo-assisted (pressure hydraulic system).

Tyres: 235/70 HR 15.   **Fuel tank:** 23.5 Imp. gall (107 litres).

Dimensions: Length 204.5 in (5194 mm), width 72 in (1829 mm), height 59.8 in (1519 mm), wheelbase 120.1 in (3050 mm).

Unladen weight: 5200 lb (2359 kg).

Performance *Autocar* test: Maximum speed 126 mph (203 km/h); 0 to 60 mph (100 km/h) 9.7 sec. Fuel consumption at constant 75 mph (120 km/h): 14.6 mpg; overall test, 12.3 mpg.

Features: Hood folds easily down, but tonneau cover is fiddly to install. Magnificent motoring with hood down, at least for those in front; rather breezy in rear. Beautifully appointed.

Identity: In the last edition, the stretched limousine version of the Silver Spirit was featured; but this was a special conversion carried out at great cost. For most buyers looking for the ultimate in luxury travel, it is this model, the standard Silver Spirit, which is prime choice.

Engine: Front-mounted longitudinal V8-cylinder with alloy blocks and heads. Pushrod ohv; hydraulic tappets. Twin SU carbs. Bore 104.1 mm, stroke 99.1 mm; capacity 6750 cc. Power and torque—no data revealed by Rolls-Royce. Compression 9.0-to-1.

Transmission: Rear-wheel drive; three-speed manual gearbox; GM automatic transmission with Rolls-Royce modifications and electric column-mounted selector. Top gear speed at 1000 rpm: 26.3 mph (42.3 km/h).

Suspension: Front, independent, wishbones and coil springs; telescopic dampers. Anti-roll bar. Rear, independent, trailing arms, coil springs and hydro-pneumatic auxiliary springs with self-levelling provision; telescopic dampers. Anti-roll bar. Power assistance: standard.

Steering: Rack and pinion. Power assistance: standard.

Brakes: Vented discs front, solid discs rear, servo-assisted.

Tyres: 235/70 HR 15.   **Fuel tank:** 23.5 Imp. gall (107 litres).

Dimensions: Length 207.4 in (5270 mm), width 72 in (1829 mm), height 58.7 in (1490 mm), wheelbase 120.5 in (3060 mm).

Unladen weight: 4950 lb (2245 kg).

Performance *Autocar* test: Maximum speed 119 mph (192 km/h); 0 to 60 mph (100 km/h) 10.0 sec. Fuel consumption at constant 75 mph (120 km/h): 16.1 mpg; overall test, 14.0 mpg.

Features: Superbly comfortable and quiet saloon, with impressive acceleration and relaxed cruising at high speeds. Sumptuous finish and lavish equipment, including electric seat adjustment.

Identity: Under the skin, the Rover 213 is pure Honda Ballade. Launched 1984, this Rover is the successor to the Triumph Acclaim, which was the first product of the association between Austin Rover and the Japanese manufacturer. Vanden Plas distinguishable by silver coloured grille.

Engine: Front-mounted, transverse, four-cylinder with overhead camshaft, three valves per cylinder; aluminium alloy head. Bore 74 mm, stroke 78 mm; capacity 1342 cc. Power 70 bhp (52 kW) at 6000 rpm; torque 77 lb ft (105 Nm) at 3500 rpm. Compression 8.7-to-1.

Transmission: Front-wheel drive; five-speed manual gearbox. Top gear speed at 1000 rpm: 20.8 mph (33.4 km/h).

Suspension: Front, independent, MacPherson struts with co-axial torsion bars; telescopic dampers. Anti-roll bar. Rear, semi-independent, trailing arms with axle tube and swivelling hub bearings. Panhard rod, coil springs, telescopic dampers.

Steering: Rack and pinion. Power assistance: not available.

Brakes: Discs front, drums rear, servo-assisted.

Tyres: 165/13.   **Fuel tank:** 10.1 Imp. gall (46 litres).

Dimensions: Length 163.6 in (4156 mm), width 63.9 in (1623 mm), height 54.3 in (1378 mm), wheelbase 96.5 in (2450 mm).

Unladen weight: 1951 lb (885 kg).

Performance *Autocar* test: Maximum speed 96 mph (154 km/h); 0 to 60 mph (100 km/h) 13.0 sec. Fuel consumption at constant 75 mph (120 km/h): 38.2 mpg; overall test, 30.9 mpg.

Features: The Rover offers more room and has better exterior appearance than its Acclaim predecessor. Disappointing ride. Vanden Plas top of the 213 range has leather seat facings and central locking.

ROVER (GB)   Vitesse

Identity: No sooner was last year's edition published, than Rover decided to make automatic transmission available, which we had said could not be ordered for the Vitesse. However, this high-performance version of the Rover remains best with the standard five-speed transmission, giving very high gearing for fast, economical cruising. New at Birmingham 1982.

Engine: Front-mounted V8-cylinder with all-alloy construction and hydraulic tappets. Lucas L electronic fuel injection. Bore 88.9 mm, stroke 71.1 mm; capacity 3528 cc. Power 190 bhp (142 kW) at 5280 rpm; torque 220 lb ft (304 Nm) at 4000 rpm. Comp. 9.75-to-1.

Transmission: Rear-wheel drive; five-speed manual gearbox. Three-speed automatic transmission optional. Final drive ratio 3.08-to-1. Top gear speed at 1000 rpm: 29.4 mph (47.3 km/h).

Suspension: Front, independent, MacPherson struts; coil springs and telescopic dampers. Anti-roll bar. Rear, torque tube live axle, with varying rate coil springs and Watts linkage; self-levelling damper units.

Steering: Rack and pinion. Power assistance: standard, varies with speed.

Brakes: Vented discs front, drums rear, servo-assisted.

Tyres: 205/60 VR 15.   **Fuel tank:** 14.5 Imp. gall (66 litres).

Dimensions: Length 186.3 in (4727 mm), width 69.6 in (1768 mm), height 53.4 in (1355 mm), wheelbase 110.8 in (2815 mm).

Unladen weight: 3173 lb (1439 kg).

Performance *Autocar* test: Maximum speed 130 mph (209 km/h); 0 to 60 mph (100 km/h) 7.6 sec. Fuel consumption at constant 75 mph (120 km/h); 30.1 mpg; overall test, 21.8 mpg.

Features: One of the fastest five-seater production cars, and still with the functional five-door body of all Rovers, Sports seats, trip computer.

Identity: So well-received was the Saab convertible at Frankfurt 1983 that Saab decided to put it into production. Availability likely early 1986. Based on the 900 Turbo, but with 16-valve engine, it has folding hood with clever arrangement for the glass rear window to wind down into a recess in the boot.

Engine: Front-mounted transverse four-cylinder with twin overhead camshafts and 16 valves. Garrett turbocharger. Bore 90 mm, stroke 78 mm; capacity 1985 cc. Power 180 bhp (132 kW) at 5500 rpm; torque 199 lb ft (275 Nm) at 3000 rpm. Compression 8.5-to-1.

Transmission: Front-wheel drive; five-speed manual gearbox; final drive ratio 4.21-to-1. Top gear speed at 1000 rpm: 24.4 mph (39.2 km/h).

Suspension: Front, independent, wishbones and coil springs; telescopic dampers. Anti-roll bar. Rear, dead beam axle on four trailing links with Panhard rod; coil springs and telescopic dampers.

Steering: Rack and pinion. Power assistance: standard.

Brakes: Discs front and rear, servo-assisted.

Tyres: 195/60 HR 15.   **Fuel tank:** 13.9 Imp. gall (63 litres).

Dimensions: Length 186.6 in (4739 mm), width 66.5 in (1690 mm), height 55.9 in (1420 mm), wheelbase 99.4 in (2525 mm).

Unladen weight: 2612 lb (1185 kg).

Performance (Works): Maximum speed 130 mph (209 km/h); 0 to 60 mph (100 km/h) 8.3 sec. Fuel consumption at constant 75 mph (120 km/h): 30.4 mpg.

Features: Handsomely-styled four-seater convertible which will be a welcome addition to the open car market when it arrives next year. With its very strong construction, the Saab should prove a sturdy convertible.

Identity: The Saab 9000 Turbo 16V was announced at Geneva 1984. A roomy, well-equipped high-performance car it becomes the new flagship of the Swedish manufacturer.

Engine: Front-mounted transverse four-cylinder with light alloy, cross-flow cylinder head. Garrett AiResearch turbocharger with anti-knock sensor. Bore 90 mm, stroke 78 mm; capacity 1985 cc. Power 175 bhp (129 kW) at 5300 rpm; torque 201 lb ft (272 Nm) at 3000 rpm. Compression 9.0-to-1.

Transmission: Front-wheel drive; five-speed manual gearbox transversely mounted on left of engine. Top gear speed at 1000 rpm: 26.6 mph (42.9 km/h).

Suspension: Front, independent, MacPherson struts, coil springs and gas-filled telescopic dampers. Anti-roll bar. Rear, rigid axle, twin longitudinal leading and trailing arms, coil springs and gas-filled telescopic dampers. Anti-roll bar.

Steering: Rack and pinion. Power assistance: standard.

Brakes: Ventilated discs front, discs rear, servo-assisted.

Tyres: 195/60 R15.   **Fuel tank:** 15 Imp. gall (68 litres).

Dimensions: Length 181.9 in (4620 mm), width 69.4 in (1764 mm), height 55.9 in (1420 mm), wheelbase 105.2 in (2672 mm).

Unladen weight: 2802 lb (1271 kg).

Performance (Works): Maximum speed 135 mph (217 km/h); 0 to 60 mph (100 km/h) 8.3 sec. Fuel consumption at constant 75 mph (120 km/h): 31.0 mpg.

Features: Long wheelbase and wide track make this a roomy, comfortable saloon, but with colossal performance from the turbocharged engine. High level of equipment.

Identity: New Spanish car of international design. Porsche worked with Seat on the engine and gearbox, Giugiaro of Italy styled the body, and Karman of Germany designed it. New concept for small two-door hatchback; 120,000 a year to be built, and distributed by Volkswagen. Choice of L, GL or GLX trim, and 1.2, 1.5 or 1.7 diesel engines. 1.5 details follow.

Engine: Front-mounted transverse four-cylinder with belt-driven ohc. Weber carb with varying cam drive to accelerator pump. Bore 83 mm, stroke 67.5 mm; capacity 1461 cc. Power 85 bhp (63 kW) at 5600 rpm; torque 84 lb ft (116 Nm) at 3500 rpm. Comp. 10.5-to-1.

Transmission: Front-wheel drive; five-speed manual gearbox; final drive 3.74-to-1 for 1.5 model, 4.29 on other two. Top gear speed at 1000 rpm: 24.5 mph (39.4 km/h).

Suspension: Front, independent, MacPherson struts and coil springs; telescopic dampers. Anti-roll bar. Rear, independent, swinging arms and transverse leaf spring. Telescopic dampers.

Steering: Rack and pinion. Power assistance: not available.

Brakes: Discs front, drums rear, servo-assisted.

Tyres: 165 SR 14.

Dimensions: Length 143.2 in (3638 mm), width 63.3 in (1609 mm), height 54.9 in (1394 mm), wheelbase 96.3 in (2448 mm).

Unladen weight: 2039 lb (925 kg).

Performance (Works): Maximum speed 109 mph (175 km/h); 0 to 60 mph (100 km/h) 12.2 sec. Fuel consumption at constant 75 mph (120 km/h): 44.1 mpg.

Features: Promising new design, due on British market 1985. GLX is well-equipped; other models less comprehensive.

SKODA (CS)   120 Rapid Cabriolet

Identity: Skoda are working hard to produce a front-engined model; but there was still no sign of it as we went to press—just the old rear-engined design of limited merit, other than cheapness. The two-door Rapid Coupé was introduced Frankfurt 1981, and mechanically similar to 120LSE except for rear suspension by trailing arms instead of the dubious principle of swing axles.

Engine: Front-mounted longitudinal four-cylinder with pushrod ohv. Alloy block. Jikov twin-choke carb. Radiator at front. Bore 72 mm, stroke 72 mm; capacity 1174 cc. Power 58 bhp (43 kW) at 5200 rpm; torque 67 lb ft (49 Nm) at 3250 rpm. Compression 8.5-to-1.

Transmission: Rear-wheel drive; four-speed manual gearbox; no five-speed or automatic options. Final drive 4.22-to-1. Top gear speed at 1000 rpm: 16.7 mph (26.9 km/h).

Suspension: Front, independent, wishbones and coil springs; telescopic dampers. Anti-roll bar. Rear, independent, semi-trailing arms, coil springs and telescopic dampers.

Steering: Rack and pinion. Power assistance: not available.

Brakes: Discs front, drums rear, servo-assisted.

Tyres: 165 SR 13.   **Fuel tank:** 8.4 Imp. gall (38 litres).

Dimensions: Length 164.5 in (4175 mm), width 63.4 in (1610 mm), height 53 in (1345 mm), wheelbase 94.5 in (2400 mm).

Unladen weight: 2016 lb (915 kg).

Performance (Works): Maximum speed 93 mph (150 km/h); 0 to 60 mph (100 km/h) 17 sec. Fuel consumption at constant 75 mph (120 km/h): 34.5 mpg.

Features: Black vinyl top with glass sunroof. Four halogen headlamps. Sports gear knob and rev counter. Radio with stereo cassette standard. Poor finish and unrefined machinery, but very low price compensates.

156

SUBARU (J)　　　　1800GLF 4WD Hatchback

Identity: Although the new L-Series has been introduced (see page 158), the former model with four-wheel drive remains in Subaru line-up. Saloon, hatchback and estate are available, and there is also an automatic transmission option.

Engine: Front-mounted longitudinal four-cylinder with horizontally-opposed layout; central camshaft. Alloy construction for heads and block. Bore 92 mm, stroke 67 mm; capacity 1782 cc. Power 84 bhp (63 kW) at 5600 rpm; torque 97 lb ft (134 Nm) at 3600 rpm. Compression 8.7-to-1.

Transmission: Four-wheel drive; four-speed manual gearbox; normal drive to front wheels; selectable drive to rear wheels. Top gear speed at 1000 rpm: 19.1 mph (30.7 km/h).

Suspension: Front, independent, MacPherson struts, coil springs and telescopic dampers. Anti-roll bar. Rear, independent, semi-trailing arms and torsion bars; telescopic dampers.

Steering: Rack and pinion. Power assistance: optional.

Brakes: Discs front, drums rear, servo-assisted.

Tyres: 155 SR 13.　　　**Fuel tank:** 13.2 Imp. gall (60 litres).

Dimensions: Length 163.6 in (4155 mm), width 63.8 in (1620 mm), height 56.9 in (1445 mm), wheelbase 96.3 in (2446 mm).

Unladen weight: 2039 lb (925 kg).

Performance *Autocar* test: Maximum speed 90 mph (145 km/h); 0 to 60 mph (100 km/h) 16.3 sec. Fuel consumption at constant 75 mph (120 km/h): 28.1 mpg; overall test, 28.1 mpg.

Features: Surprisingly rugged car, intended for hard work. Frameless glass door windows. Oblong headlamps with clear glass indicators alongside. Rather pronounced front overhang and severe understeer, but handling acceptable in view of the impressive cross-country ability.

SUBARU (J)   L-series 1.8 GTi

Identity: Smart, new model range from Subaru for the medium-size saloon car market launched Birmingham 1984. Initially available with only front-wheel drive, powered by the 1.8-litre engine in either carb. or fuel injected form (detailed below).

Engine: Front-mounted flat four-cylinder with separate, belt-driven overhead camshafts for each bank; hydraulic tappets. Bore 92 mm, stroke 67 mm; capacity 1781 cc. Power 108.5 bhp (81 kW) at 6000 rpm; torque 104.8 lb ft (142 Nm) at 3600 rpm. Compression 10.0-to-1.

Transmission: Front-wheel drive; five-speed manual gearbox; three-speed automatic transmission optional. Top gear speed at 1000 rpm: 21.7 mph (34.9 km/h).

Suspension: Front, independent, MacPherson struts and coil springs; telescopic dampers. Rear, independent, semi-trailing arms and coil springs; telescopic dampers.

Steering: Rack and pinion. Power assistance: standard.

Brakes: Ventilated discs front, drum rear, servo-assisted.

Tyres: 175/70 HR-13.   **Fuel tank:** 9.9 Imp. gall (45 litres).

Dimensions: Length 172.0 in (4370 mm), width 65.3 in (1660 mm), height 54.5 in (1385 mm), wheelbase 97.2 in (2470 mm).

Unladen weight: 2227 lb (1010 kg).

Performance (est.): Maximum speed 100 mph (160 km/h). Fuel consumption at constant 75 mph (120 km/h): 36.2 mpg.

Features: High levels of standard equipment for the L-series Subaru include tilting steering wheel, central locking and automatic rear seat belts. Optional extras include electric windows, glass sunroof and trip computer.

SUZUKI (J)   Alto

Identity: Fascinating and neatly engineered Japanese baby car. Two-door with lift-up rear hatch. Very economical. Some markets also get four-door 543 cc saloon (Fronte), and the 970 cc coupé (Cervo).

Engine: Front-mounted three-cylinder with belt-driven ohc. Mikuni-Solex carb. Alloy head. Bore 68.5 mm, stroke 72 mm; capacity 796 cc. Power 39 bhp (29 kW) at 5500 rpm; torque 43 lb ft (60 Nm) at 3000 rpm. Compression 9.5-to-1.

Transmission: Front-wheel drive; four-speed manual gearbox. Final drive ratio 4.35-to-1. Top gear speed at 1000 rpm: 14.7 mph (23.7 km/h).

Suspension: Front, independent, MacPherson struts and coil springs; telescopic dampers. Anti-roll bar. Rear, dead beam axle on semi-elliptic leaf springs. Telescopic dampers. Coupé has independent rear suspension.

Steering: Rack and pinion. Power assistance: not available.

Brakes: Drums front and rear; front discs optional.

Tyres: 145/70 SR 12.   **Fuel tank:** 6 Imp. gall (27 litres).

Dimensions: Length 129.7 in (3294 mm), width 55.3 in (1405 mm), height 52.6 in (1336 mm), wheelbase 84.7 in (2151 mm).

Unladen weight: 1389 lb (630 kg).

Performance *Autocar* test: Maximum speed 82 mph (132 km/h); 0 to 60 mph (100 km/h) 15.8 sec. Fuel consumption at constant 75 mph (120 km/h): not achieved; 56 mph (90 km/h): 47.9 mpg; overall test, 40.1 mpg.

Features: Very basic little economy car and lacking the sure-footed refinement and handling qualities of the Mini, but quite lively and simple to drive. Neatly engineered. Automatic transmission available.

159

SUZUKI (J)   SJ410WV 4 × 4

Identity: This complex title identifies the impressive little Suzuki cross-country car. Ideal for farmers and others who need a small, compact personnel carrier with seats for no more than two, yet with four-wheel drive off-road ability.

Engine: Front-mounted four-cylinder with single belt-driven ohc. Alloy head. Front, in-line, installation. Bore 65.5 mm, stroke 72 mm; capacity 970 cc. Power 47 bhp (35 kW) at 5000 rpm; torque 61 lb ft (84 Nm) at 3000 rpm. Compression 8.8-to-1.

Transmission: Four-wheel drive; four-speed manual gearbox. Normal drive to rear wheels; four-wheel drive selector adds front drive. Low-ratio transfer gearbox for severe conditions. Top gear speed at 1000 rpm: 17.9 mph (28.8 km/h).

Suspension: Front, live axle on semi-elliptic leaf springs. Telescopic dampers. Rear, live axle on semi-elliptic leaf springs. Telescopic dampers.

Steering: Rack and pinion. Power assistance: not available.

Brakes: Discs front, drums rear.

Tyres: 195 SR 15.   **Fuel tank:** 8.8 Imp. gall (40 litres).

Dimensions: Length 135 in (3430 mm), width 57.5 in (1460 mm), height 66.5 in (1690 mm), wheelbase 80 in (2030 mm).

Unladen weight: 1830 lb (830 kg).

Performance *Autocar* test: Maximum speed 68 mph (109 km/h); 0 to 60 mph (100 km/h) too slow to measure. Fuel consumption, overall test, 25.3 mpg.

Features: Impressive cross-country ability. Easy to drive. Choice of tilt cover or hardtop. Effective utility vehicle without the heavy running costs incurred by larger 4 × 4 vehicles. Hard suspension gives very rough ride.

TALBOT (F, GB)   Horizon Pullman

Identity: First introduced 1977, the Horizon was launched as a special edition in a new up-market version of the four-door hatchback at Birmingham 1984. Based on the LS version mechanically, the Pullman has a distinctive interior and two-tone metallic paint bodywork.

Engine: Front-mounted transverse four-cylinder with aluminium alloy cylinder head. Bore 76.7 mm, stroke 78 mm; capacity 1442 cc. Power 83 bhp (62 kW) at 5600 rpm; torque 90 lb ft (122 Nm) at 3000 rpm. Compression 9.5-to-1.

Transmission: Front-wheel drive; five-speed manual gearbox. Top gear speed at 1000 rpm: 22.2 mph (35.8 km/h).

Suspension: Front, independent, wishbones and longitudinal torsion bars; telescopic dampers. Anti-roll bar. Rear, independent, trailing arms and coil springs, telescopic dampers.

Steering: Rack and pinion. Power assistance: standard.

Brakes: Discs front, drums rear, servo-assisted.

Tyres: 175/70 SR-13.   **Fuel tank:** 9.9 Imp. gall (45 litres).

Dimensions: Length 155.9 in (3960 mm), width 66.1 in (1679 mm), height 55.5 in (1410 mm), wheelbase 99.2 in (2520 mm).

Unladen weight: 2182 lb (990 kg).

Performance (Works): Maximum speed 101 mph (162 km/h); 0 to 60 mph (100 km/h) 13.2 sec. Fuel consumption at constant 75 mph (120 km/h): 39.2 mpg.

Features: Easily distinguishable by its smart two-tone paintwork and alloy wheels, the Pullman has seats trimmed in velour. Polished wood-capped facia and four-speaker stereo radio/cassette player standard.

TALBOT (F)   Matra Murena

Identity: Unusual sports car with three-abreast seating; successor to the Bagheera model, with aerodynamic two-door hatchback body. Mid-engined layout. Available only with left-hand drive, and not imported to Britain. Choice of 1.6-litre (detailed below) or 2.2-litre engine.

Engine: Mid-mounted four-cylinder with alloy head. Pushrod ohv. Weber twin-choke carb. Transverse installation. Bore 80.6 mm, stroke 78 mm; capacity 1592 cc. Power 90 bhp (67.5 kW) at 5600 rpm; torque 96 lb ft (132 Nm) at 3200 rpm. Compression 9.45-to-1.

Transmission: Rear-wheel drive; five-speed manual gearbox. Final drive ratio 4.77-to-1. Top gear speed at 1000 rpm: 19.7 mph (31.7 km/h).

Suspension: Front, independent, wishbones and torsion bars; telescopic dampers. Anti-roll bar. Rear, independent, semi-trailing arms and coil springs; telescopic dampers. Anti-roll bar.

Steering: Rack and pinion. Power assistance: not available.

Brakes: Discs front and rear, servo-assisted.

Tyres: 185/60 HR 14 (front), 195/60 HR 14 (rear).   **Fuel tank:** 12.3 Imp. gall (56 litres).

Dimensions: Length 160.2 in (4070 mm), width 68.9 in (1750 mm), height 48 in (1220 mm), wheelbase 95.9 in (2435 mm).

Unladen weight: 2204 lb (1000 kg).

Performance (Works): Maximum speed 113 mph (182 km/h); 0 to 60 mph (100 km/h) 11.8 sec. Fuel consumption, 38.7 mpg (at constant 75 mph, 120 km/h).

Features: Glass fibre body on steel chassis. Electronic ignition introduced Paris 1982, and latest version is identified by internal door pockets. Velour upholstery; 2.2 has central locking.

Identity: Functional-looking and quite spacious two-door semi-estate with 1442 cc engine and front-drive. Distinctive body style with unusual layout of lamps including two big fog lamps set in front bumper. External visor over top of windscreen. Rancho was launched Geneva 1977; still on sale much as original form.

Engine: Front-mounted transverse four-cylinder with alloy head, side camshaft and pushrod valve gear. Weber carb. Bore 76.7 mm, stroke 78 mm; capacity 1442 cc. Power 79 bhp (59 kW) at 5600 rpm; torque 85 lb ft (118 Nm) at 3000 rpm. Compression 9.5-to-1.

Transmission: Front-wheel drive; four-speed manual gearbox; no automatic or four-wheel drive options. Top gear speed at 1000 rpm: 18.6 mph (29.9 km/h).

Suspension: Front, independent, wishbones and longitudinal torsion bars; telescopic dampers. Anti-roll bar. Rear, independent, trailing arms and transverse torsion bars; telescopic dampers. Anti-roll bar.

Steering: Rack and pinion. Power assistance: not available.

Brakes: Discs front, drums rear, servo-assisted.

Tyres: 185/70 SR 14.   **Fuel tank:** 13.2 Imp. gall (60 litres).

Dimensions: Length 169.9 in (4315 mm), width 65.6 in (1665 mm), height 68.3 in (1735 mm), wheelbase 99.3 in (2521 mm).

Unladen weight: 2491 lb (1130 kg).

Performance *Autocar* test: Maximum speed 89 mph (143 km/h); 0 to 60 mph (100 km/h) 14.9 sec. Fuel consumption at constant 75 mph (120 km/h): 25.2 mpg; overall test, 25.7 mpg.

Features: Although it looks like a cross-country car, the Rancho has only front-drive and very easily gets stuck in mud or snow; regrettably no four-wheel drive version is offered. Adaptable, roomy four-seater body with functional appeal; two side doors and tailgate.

TALBOT (GB, F)   Rapier

Identity: Two former model names were reintroduced at Birmingham 1984: Rapier and Minx. Well-known in the past these names identify improved models available in either four-door saloon or five-door hatchback guise, of the Alpine and Solara. The up-market version is the Rapier. All models are powered by the 1.6-litre engine and have five-speed gearboxes.

Engine: Front-mounted transverse four-cylinder with alloy cylinder head and pushrod ohv. Bore 80.6 mm, stroke 78 mm; capacity 1592 cc. Power 90 bhp (67 kW) at 5400 rpm; torque 101 lb ft (137 Nm) at 3800 rpm. Compression 9.35-to-1.

Transmission: Front-wheel drive; five-speed manual gearbox. Top gear speed at 1000 rpm: 21.3 mph (34.3 km/h).

Suspension: Front, independent, wishbones and torsion bars; telescopic dampers. Anti-roll bar. Rear, independent, trailing arms, coil springs and telescopic dampers. Anti-roll bar.

Steering: Rack and pinion. Power assistance: standard.

Brakes: Discs front, drums rear, servo-assisted.

Tyres: 165/82 SR-13.   **Fuel tank:** 12.75 Imp. gall (58 litres).

Dimensions: Length 173 in (4393 mm), width 66.1 in (1680 mm), height 54.7 in (1390 mm), wheelbase 102.5 in (2604 mm).

Unladen weight: 2292 lb (1040 kg).

Performance (Works): Maximum speed 104 mph (167 km/h); 0 to 60 mph (100 km/h) 12.7 sec. Fuel consumption at constant 75 mph (120 km/h): 36.2 mpg,

Features: Same mechanically as the Minx but with better equipment. Distinguishable by new radiator grille in body colour. Deep side body mouldings. Alloy wheels and metallic paint. Velour seats and trim.

TALBOT (F, GB)   Samba Cabriolet

Identity: Familiar chunky shape of Talbot's charming little economy car, in convertible guise with fixed roll bar. Launched October 1981, and on the British market, Birmingham 1982.

Engine: Front-mounted four-cylinder with transverse mounting, and inclined rearward at 72 deg angle. Alloy head and block. Chain-driven ohc. Bore 75 mm, stroke 77 mm; capacity 1361 cc. Power 71 bhp (53 kW) at 6000 rpm; torque 77 lb ft (107 Nm) at 3000 rpm. Compression 9.3-to-1.

Transmission: Front-wheel drive; four-speed gearbox, all indirect. Final drive 3.56-to-1. Top gear speed at 1000 rpm: 20.0 mph (32.2 km/h).

Suspension: Front, independent, MacPherson struts and coil springs; telescopic dampers; anti-roll bar. Rear, independent, trailing arms, coil springs and telescopic dampers.

Steering: Rack and pinion. Power assistance: not available.

Brakes: Discs front, drums rear, servo-assisted.

Tyres: 165/70 SR 13.   **Fuel tank:** 8.8 Imp. gall (40 litres).

Dimensions: Length 138 in (3505 mm), width 60 in (1530 mm), height 53.5 in (1360 mm), wheelbase 92 in (2340 mm).

Unladen weight: 1872 lb (850 kg).

Performance *Autocar* test: Maximum speed 93 mph (150 km/h); 0 to 60 mph (100 km/h) 12.5 sec. Fuel consumption at constant 75 mph (120 km/h): 40.4 mpg; overall test, 35.3 mpg.

Features: Welcome addition to all-too-limited choice of open cars; easy to drive, good handling, hood quite simple to put up or down, and outstanding economy. Rather a lot of wind noise when hood is up.

TOYOTA (J)   **Camry 1.8 turbo diesel**

Identity: Toyota's saloon flagship for the UK. Similar in looks and mechanical arrangement to the Carina, the Camry is longer. Engine options are 1.8-litre petrol, 2.0-litre petrol with fuel injection and 1.8-litre turbocharged diesel. Five-speed gearboxes are standard; four-speed automatic available on each model except diesel.

Engine: Front-mounted transverse, four-cylinder diesel with aluminium alloy head, cast iron block. Toyota's own turbocharger. Bore 83 mm, stroke 85 mm; capacity 1839 cc. Power 73 bhp (54 kW) at 4500 rpm; torque 107 lb ft (145 Nm) at 2600 rpm. Compression 22.5-to-1.

Transmission: Front-wheel drive; five-speed manual gearbox; automatic transmission optional. Top gear speed at 1000 rpm: 23.5 mph (37.8 km/h).

Suspension: Front, independent, MacPherson struts, coil springs; telescopic dampers. Rear, independent, MacPherson struts, coil springs; telescopic dampers. Anti-roll bar.

Steering: Rack and pinion. Power assistance: standard.

Brakes: Discs front, drums rear, servo-assisted.

Tyres: 185/70 HR 13.   **Fuel tank:** 12.1 Imp. gall (55 litres).

Dimensions: Length 173.8 in (4414 mm), width 66.5 in (1689 mm), height 54.9 in (1394 mm), wheelbase 102.4 in (2600 mm).

Unladen weight: 2559 lb (4460 kg).

Performance *Autocar* test: Maximum speed 99 mph (160 km/h); 0 to 60 mph (100 km/h) 13.5 sec. Fuel consumption at constant 75 mph (120 km/h): 39.2 mpg; overall test, 34.6 mpg.

Features: Very good performance for a diesel, which, with light and easy controls, makes this a pleasant car to drive. Good level of equipment, the most lavish being on the 2.0 GLi version.

TOYOTA (J)   Carina 1.6 GL

Identity: Available as a four-door saloon or three-door Liftback, the Carina falls into Toyota's mid-range. Now in Carina II form, the exterior appearance has been improved. Front-wheel drive is available with 1.6-litre petrol or 2.0-litre diesel engine.

Engine: Front-mounted transverse, four-cylinder with aluminium alloy head and block. Bore 81 mm, stroke 71 mm; capacity 1587 cc. Power 83 bhp (61.8 kW) at 5600 rpm; torque 96 lb ft (130 Nm) at 3600 rpm. Compression 9.3-to-1.

Transmission: Front-wheel drive; five-speed manual gearbox; four-speed automatic available. Top gear speed at 1000 rpm: 20.5 mph (161 km/h).

Suspension: Front, independent, MacPherson struts, coil springs; telescopic dampers. Anti-roll bar. Rear, independent, MacPherson struts, coil springs, dual lower links; telescopic dampers. Anti-roll bar.

Steering: Rack and pinion. Power assistance: standard.

Brakes: Discs front, drums rear, servo-assisted.

Tyres: 165 SR-13.   **Fuel tank:** 12.1 Imp. gall (55 litres).

Dimensions: Length 170 in (4330 mm), width 65.7 in (1670 mm), height 53.7 in (1365 mm), wheelbase 99 in (2515 mm).

Unladen weight: 2149 lb (974 kg).

Performance *Autocar* test: Maximum speed 101 mph (162 km/h); 0 to 60 mph (100 km/h) 12.6 sec. Fuel consumption at constant 75 mph (120 km/h): 39.2 mpg; overall test, 35.6 mpg.

Features: Very economical for a petrol-engined car. In Liftback form the Carina II has split rear seats and a good load-carrying capacity. Light controls.

TOYOTA (J)   Corolla 1600 GT Coupé

Identity: Exciting car in the Toyota range. First introduced with rear-wheel drive (details below). From March 1985, the new front-drive version replaces the original 1600 GT. Power unit is the excellent 1.6-litre Twin Cam 16-valve engine.

Engine: Front-mounted four-cylinder with four valves per cylinder, electronic fuel injection. Bore 81 mm, stroke 77 mm; capacity 1587 cc. Power 124 bhp (92 kW) at 6600 rpm; torque 105 lb ft (142 Nm) at 5200 rpm. Compression 10.0-to-1.

Transmission: Rear-wheel drive; five-speed manual gearbox. Top gear speed at 1000 rpm: 18.39 mph (29.6 km/h).

Suspension: Front, independent, MacPherson struts, lower links, coil springs; telescopic dampers. Anti-roll bar. Rear, live axle, trailing arms, coil springs and Panhard rod; telescopic dampers. Anti-roll bar.

Steering: Rack and pinion. Power assistance: not available.

Brakes: Discs front, drums rear, servo-assisted.

Tyres: 185/70 HR-13.   **Fuel tank:** 11.0 Imp. gall (50 litres).

Dimensions: Length 164.6 in (4181 mm), width 64 in (1626 mm), height 52.6 in (1354 mm), wheelbase 94.5 in (2400 mm).

Unladen weight: 2156 lb (978 kg).

Performance *Autocar* test: Maximum speed 118 mph (190 km/h); 0 to 60 mph (100 km/h) 8.6 sec. Fuel consumption, overall test, 27.0 mpg.

Features: Superb performance and response. Very successful Group A rally car. Fun to drive, but the pay-off is the very harsh ride. Sporty appearance with front air dam and rear spoiler.

TOYOTA (J)   Celica 2.0 XT Coupé

Identity: Sporting four-seater available as Coupé (illustrated) or liftback. New version introduced on British market February 1984 has pop-up headlamps concealed behind extensions of radiator grille. Automatic option mentioned below is only for liftback version.

Engine: Front-mounted four-cylinder with chain-driven ohc, electronic ignition, and Aisin twin-choke carb. Iron block, alloy head. Bore 84 mm, stroke 89 mm; capacity 1972 cc. Power 103 bhp (77 kW) at 5000 rpm; torque 116 lb ft (160 Nm) at 4000 rpm. Compression 9.0-to-1.

Transmission: Rear-wheel drive; five-speed gearbox standard, with Hypoid 3.91-to-1 final drive. Four-speed automatic available. Top gear speed at 1000 rpm: 21.1 mph (34 km/h).

Suspension: Front, independent, MacPherson struts; coil springs and telescopic dampers; anti-roll bar. Rear, independent, semi-trailing arms and coil springs; telescopic dampers; anti-roll bar.

Steering: Rack and pinion. Power assistance: standard, effort speed-related.

Brakes: Discs front, drums rear, servo-assisted.

Tyres: 185/70 SR 14.   **Fuel tank:** 13.4 Imp. gall (61 litres).

Dimensions: Length 170.6 in (4435 mm), width 65.6 in (1665 mm), height 52 in (1320 mm), wheelbase 98.4 in (2500 mm).

Unladen weight: 2576 lb (1170 kg).

Performance *Autocar* test: Maximum speed 109 mph (175 km/h); 0 to 60 mph (100 km/h) 10.5 sec. Fuel consumption at constant 75 mph (120 km/h): 31.5 mpg; overall test, 25.2 mpg.

Features: Very pleasing touring car, with emphasis more on the comfort side than on sporting behaviour, but very well equipped.

TOYOTA (J)   Corolla GL Liftback

Identity: Replacement for previous best-seller in the world, again aiming high with competent design and much more modern concept featuring front-wheel drive and transverse engine. Choice of four-door saloon, or five-door hatchback. Slightly larger than previous Corolla.

Engine: Front-mounted transverse in-line four-cylinder with single ohc. Alloy head. Aisin twin-choke carb, with automatic choke. Bore 76 mm, stroke 71.4 mm; capacity 1295 cc. Power 69 bhp (51 kW) at 6000 rpm; torque 75 lb ft (104 Nm) at 3800 rpm. Compression 9.3-to-1.

Transmission: Front-wheel drive; five-speed manual gearbox; Aisin Warner automatic with three speeds and torque converter lock-up optional. Top gear speed at 1000 rpm: 19.8 mph (31.9 km/h); automatic 19.7 mph (31.7 km/h).

Suspension: Front, independent, MacPherson struts; offset coil springs and telescopic dampers. Anti-roll bar. Rear, independent, MacPherson struts; offset coil springs and telescopic dampers.

Steering: Rack and pinion. Power assistance: not available.

Brakes: Discs front, drums rear, servo-assisted.

Tyres: 155 SR 13.   **Fuel tank:** 11 Imp. gall (50 litres).

Dimensions: Length 163 in (4135 mm), width 64.4 in (1635 mm), height 54.5 in (1384 mm), wheelbase 95.7 in (2430 mm).

Unladen weight: 1995 lb (905 kg).

Performance *Autocar* test: Maximum speed 92 mph (148 km/h); 0 to 60 mph (100 km/h) 14.2 sec. Fuel consumption at constant 75 mph (120 km/h): 37.2 mpg; overall test, 30.2.

Features: Easy car to handle, with consistent slight understeer. Liftback costs more, but is appreciably more economical.

Identity: Probably one of the most exciting small cars to be released in the last 12 months. Toyota's MR2—Midship Runabout, 2-seater—is an affordable new sports car. Powered by the excellent 1.6-litre Twin Cam engine, also in the Corolla GT but positioned transversely just ahead of the rear wheels.

Engine: Mid-mounted transverse four-cylinder with twin overhead camshafts; 16 valves. Bore 81 mm, stroke 77 mm; capacity 1587 cc. Power 122 bhp (91 kW) at 6600 rpm; torque 104 lb ft (142 Nm) at 5000 rpm. Compression 10.0-to-1.

Transmission: Rear-wheel drive; five-speed manual gearbox. Top gear speed at 1000 rpm: 21.4 mph (34.4 km/h).

Suspension: Front, independent, MacPherson struts and coil springs; telescopic dampers. Anti-roll bar. Rear, independent, MacPherson struts, coil springs and telescopic dampers. Anti-roll bar.

Steering: Rack and pinion. Power assistance: not available.

Brakes: Ventilated discs front and rear, servo-assisted.

Tyres: 185/60 R-14.   **Fuel tank:** 9.0 Imp. gall (41 litres).

Dimensions: Length 154.5 in (3925 mm), width 65.5 in (1665 mm), height 49.2 in (1250 mm), wheelbase 91.3 in (2320 mm).

Unladen weight: 2149 lb (975 kg).

Performance (Works): Maximum speed 130 mph (209 km/h); 0 to 60 mph (100 km/h) 8.0 sec. No fuel consumption data available.

Features: With a front/rear weight distribution of 45/55 this mid-engined sports car should possess excellent handling characteristics which, in conjunction with the responsive Toyota Twin Cam engine, should make it very enjoyable to drive.

TOYOTA (J)   Model F Space-Cruiser

Identity: Fascinating new concept of car, combining the roominess of a van with car-type interior trim and comfort. An ideal car for general company duties. Two rows of seats in the body of the vehicle plus the front seats carry eight in total. The seats can be refolded as a bed. Two front doors, top-hinged tailgate, and sliding nearside door.

Engine: Front-mounted longitudinal four-cylinder with alloy head chain-driven side camshaft and pushrod ohv. Aisin carb. Bore 86 mm, stroke 78 mm; capacity 1812 cc. Power 78 bhp (58 kW) at 4800 rpm; torque 103 lb ft (142 Nm) at 3400 rpm. Compression 8.8-to-1.

Transmission: Rear-wheel drive; five-speed manual gearbox; automatic four-speed Aisin-Warner automatic transmission optional. Top gear speed at 1000 rpm: 19.9 mph (32.0 km/h).

Suspension: Front, independent, wishbones and torsion bars; telescopic dampers. Anti-roll bar. Rear, live axle on trailing arms; coil springs and telescopic dampers. Anti-roll bar.

Steering: Recirculating ball. Power assistance: standard.

Brakes: Discs front, drums rear, servo-assisted.

Tyres: 175 SR 14.   **Fuel tank:** 12.1 Imp. gall (55 litres).

Dimensions: Length 168.7 in (4285 mm), width 65.7 in (1670 mm), height 71.4 in (1815 mm), wheelbase 87.9 in (2235 mm).

Unladen weight: 2910 lb (1320 kg).

Performance (Works): Maximum speed 84 mph (135 km/h); 0 to 60 mph (100 km/h) 18 sec. Fuel consumption at constant 75 mph (120 km/h): 24.1 mpg.

Features: Rear seat folds for extra luggage space. Attractively furnished and easy access through sliding side door. Tilting glass moonroof over front seats, and electric sliding sunroof over centre of body. Well equipped with stereo radio/cassette and twin heater controls.

172

TOYOTA (J)   Supra 2.8i

Identity: Sporting version of the Celica Coupé, launched in Britain August 1982. Similar body, but with different front, and pop-up headlamps in place of Celica's 'tilt' lamps. Powerful six-cylinder injection engine gives vigorous performance to rival top GT cars. Automatic option added February 1984.

Engine: Front-mounted six-cylinder with twin ohc driven by toothed belt. Breakerless ignition and Nippondenso injection. Bore 83 mm, stroke 85 mm; capacity 2759 cc. Power 168 bhp (125 kW) at 5600 rpm; torque 169 lb ft (286 Nm) at 4600 rpm. Compression 8.8-to-1.

Transmission: Rear-wheel drive; five-speed manual gearbox. Four-speed automatic, with torque converter lock-up in fourth, optional from Feb. 1984. Top gear speed at 1000 rpm: 22.6 mph (36.4 km/h).

Suspension: Front, independent, MacPherson struts; coil springs and telescopic dampers. Anti-roll bar. Rear, independent, semi-trailing arms; coil springs and telescopic dampers. Anti-roll bar.

Steering: Rack and pinion. Power assistance: standard.

Brakes: Vented discs front, drums rear, servo-assisted.

Tyres: 195/70 VR 14.   **Fuel tank:** 13.4 Imp. gall (61 litres).

Dimensions: Length 182 in (4620 mm), width 66.3 in (1685 mm), height 51.8 in (1315 mm), wheelbase 103 in (2615 mm).

Unladen weight: 2870 lb (1302 kg).

Performance *Autocar* test: Maximum speed 131 mph (211 km/h); 0 to 60 mph (100 km/h) 8.7 sec. Fuel consumption at constant 75 mph (120 km/h): 27.4 mpg; overall test, 19.4 mpg.

Features: Impressive facia layout with 'half moon' instruments. Two-door hatchback body, with divided, folding, rear seats. Well-equipped and rewarding to drive.

TOYOTA (J)   Tercel 4WD

Identity: Very good all-purpose utility car, offering combination of estate car carrying capacity, quite good road performance, and acceptable off-road ability. A competitor for the 'car that won't get stuck' market pioneered by Subaru.

Engine: Front-mounted in-line four-cylinder with longitudinal installation. Belt-driven ohc. Alloy head. Bore 77.5 mm, stroke 77 mm; capacity 1453 cc. Power 70 bhp (52 kW) at 5600 rpm; torque 78 lb ft (108 Nm) at 3800 rpm. Compression 9.1-to-1.

Transmission: Four-wheel drive; six-speed manual gearbox; normal drive to front wheels; rear drive selectable. Sixth gear is emergency low for very steep climbs. Top gear speed at 1000 rpm: 21.6 mph (34.7 km/h).

Suspension: Front, independent, MacPherson struts; coil springs and telescopic dampers. Rear, live axle on longitudinal links with Panhard rod. Coil springs and telescopic dampers. Anti-roll bar.

Steering: Rack and pinion. Power assistance: not available.

Brakes: Discs front, drums rear, servo-assisted.

Tyres: 156 SR 13.   **Fuel tank:** 11 Imp. gall (50 litres).

Dimensions: Length 164 in (4175 mm), width 63.5 in (1615 mm), height 59.5 in (1510 mm), wheelbase 95.7 in (2430 mm).

Unladen weight: 2138 lb (970 kg).

Performance *Autocar* test: Maximum speed 92 mph (148 km/h); 0 to 60 mph (100 km/h) 14.2 sec. Fuel consumption at constant 75 mph (120 km/h): 39.8 mpg; overall test, 29.1 mpg.

Features: Five-door estate car body with extra deep side windows at rear on each side. Selectable four-wheel drive and generous ground clearance make the Tercel 4WD surprisingly competent on soft going, and low ratio first gear gives good hill climbing ability.

TVR (GB) 390SE convertible

Identity: Using the familiar and attractive GRP-body, TVR's perform-ance model is a true 'blood and guts' sports car. Powered by a bored-out Rover 3.5-litre engine and with revised suspension, the 390SE is very fast, and retains the model's good handling.

Engine: Front-mounted in-line V8-cylinder with Cosworth pistons, gas-flowed heads and high lift camshafts. Bore 93.5 mm, stroke 77 mm; capacity 3905 cc. Power 275 bhp (205 kW) at 5500 rpm; torque 270 lb ft (366 Nm) at 3500 rpm. Compression 9.8-to-1.

Transmission: Rear-wheel drive; five-speed manual gearbox; no automatic option. Top gear speed at 1000 rpm: 26.8 mph (43.1 km/h).

Suspension: Front, independent, double wishbones and coil springs; telescopic dampers. Anti-roll bar. Rear, independent, trailing arms and fixed length drive shafts. Coil springs and telescopic dampers.

Steering: Rack and pinion. Power assistance: not available.

Brakes: Ventilated discs front, drums rear, servo-assisted.

Tyres: 225/50 VR-15.   **Fuel tank:** 14 Imp. gall (62.5 litres).

Dimensions: Length   158 in   (4013 mm),   width   68¾ in (1728 mm), height 47 in (1192 mm), wheelbase 94 in (2387 mm).

Unladen weight: 2822 lb (1280 kg).

Performance *Autocar* test: Maximum speed 144 mph (232 km/h); 0 to 60 mph (100 km/h) 5.6 sec. Fuel consumption; overall test, 21.3 mpg.

Features: Very rapid two-seater sports car. Easily removable roof panel, and rear quarter hood then folds down. Leather upholstery and walnut veneer facia.

VAUXHALL (GB, D)   Astra SR

Identity: Sister model to the European Opel Kadett, the Vauxhall Astra was completely redesigned August 1984 and has a significantly changed body shape. Available in two body styles—hatchback or estate car with three or five doors—a combination that leads to a 17 model line-up. Choice of five engines: 1.8-litre, 1.6 (in the SR, detailed below), 1.3- and 1.2- or 1.6-litre diesel.

Engine: Front-mounted transverse four-cylinder with light-alloy cross-flow head and overhead camshaft. Bore 80 mm, stroke 79.5 mm; capacity 1598 cc. Power 90 bhp (67 kW) at 5800 rpm; torque 93 lb ft (126 Nm) at 3800 rpm. Compression 9.2-to-1.

Transmission: Front-wheel drive; five-speed manual gearbox. Top gear speed at 1000 rpm: 19.76 mph (31.8 km/h).

Suspension: Front, independent, MacPherson struts and coil springs; telescopic dampers. Heavy duty rubber mountings. Anti-roll bar. Rear, compound crank dead axle, miniblock coil springs and telescopic dampers. Anti-roll bar.

Steering: Rack and pinion. Power assistance: optional.

Brakes: Discs front, drums rear, servo-assisted.

Tyres: 155 SR-13.   **Fuel tank:** 9.2 Imp. gall (42 litres).

Dimensions: Length 157.4 in (3998 mm), width 65.5 in (1664 mm), height 55.1 in (1400 mm), wheelbase 99.2 in (2520 mm).

Unladen weight: 2072 lb (940 kg).

Performance (Works): Maximum speed 114 mph (183 km/h); 0 to 60 mph (100 km/h) 11.0 sec. Fuel consumption at constant 75 mph (120 km/h): 37.7 mpg.

Features: Aerodynamic, and visually attractive new body shape. Light polypropylene nose piece and wrap around front bumper front and rear.

VAUXHALL (GB, D)

Carlton CD

Identity: Since its 1977 introduction, the Vauxhall Carlton—known as the Opel Rekord outside Britain—has been steadily improved. Latest step up for the top model, Carlton CD, was increase of engine capacity to 2197 cc at Paris 1984. 1.8- and 2.0-litre versions still available, as well as 2.3-litre diesel.

Engine: Front-mounted longitudinal four-cylinder with camshaft mounted in head, operating hydraulic tappets. Bosch LE Jetronic fuel injection. Bore 95 mm, stroke 77.5 mm; capacity 2197 cc. Power 113 bhp (85 kW) at 4800 rpm; torque 134 lb ft (185 Nm) at 2800 rpm. Compression 9.4-to-1.

Transmission: Rear-wheel drive; five-speed manual gearbox; GM three-speed automatic transmission optional. Final drive 3.45-to-1. Top gear speed at 1000 rpm: 25.1 mph (40.5 km/h).

Suspension: Front, independent, MacPherson struts and coil springs; telescopic dampers. Anti-roll bar. Rear, live axle on four trailing links with lateral track rod; coil springs and gas-filled telescopic dampers.

Steering: Recirculating ball. Power assistance: standard.

Brakes: Vented discs front, drums rear, servo-assisted. Anti-lock brakes optional on all Carlton/Rekord models.

Tyres: 185/70 HR 14. **Fuel tank:** 14.3 Imp. gall (65 litres).

Dimensions: Length 183 in (4650 mm), width 68 in (1727 mm), height 54.6 in (1387 mm), wheelbase 105 in (4134 mm).

Unladen weight: 2667 lb (1210 kg).

Performance (Works): Maximum speed 118 mph (190 km/h); 0 to 60 mph (100 km/h) 10.5 sec. Fuel consumption at constant 75 mph (120 km/h): 32.1 mpg.

Features: Anti-lock brakes become important option for all Carlton/Rekord models. Very comfortable, with generous equipment in this top CD version.

VAUXHALL (GB, D)   Cavalier 1.8 CD

Identity: Launched Birmingham 1982 was a new version of the Vauxhall engine with capacity increased to 1.8-litre, and offered in a sporting version (SRi) plus a luxury model (details follow), the CD. Engine optimized to give high torque at low revs, resulting in better pulling and economy. Both are available as saloon or hatchback.

Engine: Front-mounted transverse four-cylinder with belt-driven ohc. Hydraulic tappets. Alloy head. Bosch LE Jetronic fuel injection. Bore 84.8 mm, stroke 79.5 mm; capacity 1796 cc. Power 115 bhp (86 kW) at 5800 rpm; torque 111 lb ft (153 Nm) at 4800 rpm. Comp. 9.2-to-1.

Transmission: Front-wheel drive; five-speed manual gearbox; GM three-speed automatic transmission optional. Top gear speed at 1000 rpm: 25.3 mph (40.7 km/h).

Suspension: Front, independent, MacPherson struts; coil springs and telescopic dampers. Anti-roll bar. Rear, dead beam central joint rear axle with two link location; coil springs and telescopic dampers.

Steering: Rack and pinion. Power assistance: standard.

Brakes: Discs front, drums rear, servo-assisted.

Tyres: 185/70 HR 13.   **Fuel tank:** 13.4 Imp. gall (61 litres).

Dimensions: Length (saloon) 167.9 in (4264 mm); (hatchback) 172 in (4366 mm), width 65.7 in (1669 mm), height 54.9 in (1394 mm), wheelbase 101.3 in (2573 mm).

Unladen weight: 2337 lb (1060 kg).

Performance *Autocar* test: Maximum speed 112 mph (180 km/h); 0 to 60 mph (100 km/h) 9.3 sec. Fuel consumption at constant 75 mph (120 km/h): 37.1 mpg; overall test, 29.6 mpg.

Features: Lavishly equipped and very refined car, with headlamps wash/wipe, electric front window lifts and stereo radio/cassette player.

VAUXHALL (GB, AUS) Cavalier 1.6L Estate car

Identity: Following very successful launch of the Opel Ascona at Frankfurt 1981, in Britain as Vauxhall Cavalier, an estate car version was added two years later. Five doors and Base, L or GL trim with 1.6-litre engine only; also 1.6-litre diesel and L trim.

Engine: Front-mounted transverse four-cylinder with belt-driven ohc. Alloy head. GMF Varajet carburettor, now manual choke. Bore 80 mm, stroke 79.5 mm; capacity 1598 cc. Power 90 bhp (67 kW) at 5800 rpm; torque 93 lb ft (129 Nm) at 3800 rpm. Comp. 9.2-to-1.

Transmission: Front-wheel drive; four-speed manual gearbox; five-speed manual or three-speed automatic are options. Top gear speed at 1000 rpm: 19.4 mph (31.2 km/h).

Suspension: Front, independent, MacPherson struts and coil springs; telescopic dampers. Anti-roll bar. Rear, dead beam compound crank axle with miniblock coil springs and telescopic dampers. Anti-roll bar.

Steering: Rack and pinion. Power assistance: optional.

Brakes: Discs front, drums rear, servo-assisted.

Tyres: 165 SR 13.   **Fuel tank:** 13.2 Imp. gall (60 litres).

Dimensions: Length 170.3 in (4326 mm), width 66.4 in (1687 mm), height 53.9 in (1369 mm), wheelbase 101.5 in (2578 mm).

Unladen weight: 2299 lb (1045 kg).

Performance (Works): Maximum speed 102 mph (164 km/h); 0 to 60 mph (100 km/h) 13.5 sec. Fuel consumption at constant 75 mph (120 km/h): 34.0 mpg.

Features: Clever design for an estate car, with centre section of rear bumper mounted to lower part of tailgate, for low loading height. Deflector at top of tailgate to keep rear window clear of dirt in wet weather. Rear seat split 60/40. Many detail improvements introduced Birmingham 1984.

VAUXHALL (E)   Nova 1.2 GL Hatchback

Identity: Introduced initially as the Opel Corsa (Paris 1982), the new GM small car built exclusively in Spain came to Britain April 1983 as the Vauxhall Nova. Choice of saloon or hatchback body with 1.0- or 1.2-litre engine (detailed below), plus the SR, which has hatchback body only, and 1.3-litre engine.

Engine: Front-mounted transverse four-cylinder with alloy cross-flow head; belt-driven ohc. Pierburg carb. Bore 77.8 mm, stroke 62.9 mm; capacity 1196 cc. Power 55 bhp (41 kW) at 5600 rpm; torque 66 lb ft (91 Nm) at 2200 rpm. Compression 9.2-to-1.

Transmission: Front-wheel drive; four-speed manual gearbox; five-speed optional; no automatic option. Top gear speed at 1000 rpm: 19.3 mph (31.1 km/h).

Suspension: Front, independent, MacPherson struts and coil springs; telescopic dampers. Anti-roll bar. Rear, semi-independent, dead beam axle on trailing arms with coil springs; telescopic dampers. Torsion beam gives anti-roll effect.

Steering: Rack and pinion. Power assistance: not available.

Brakes: Discs front, drums rear, servo-assisted.

Tyres: 155/70 SR 13.   **Fuel tank:** 9.2 Imp. gall (42 litres).

Dimensions: Length 142.6 in (3622 mm), width 60.6 in (1532 mm), height 53.7 in (1364 mm), wheelbase 92.2 in (2343 mm).

Unladen weight: 1631 lb (740 kg).

Performance *Autocar* test: Maximum speed 94 mph (151 km/h); 0 to 60 mph (100 km/h) 14.2 sec. Fuel consumption at constant 75 mph (120 km/h): 43.6 mpg; overall test, 36.9 mpg.

Features: Lively performance for a 1.2-litre, and not too noisy at cruising speeds.

VAUXHALL (GB)   Senator 3.0i CD

Identity: Flagship of the Vauxhall range is the Senator saloon. The range includes two engine options, 2.5- or 3.0-litre, both with Bosch fuel injection, the third model being the luxury CD version (detailed below).

Engine: Front-mounted longitudinal six-cylinder with chain-driven camshaft. Hydraulic tappets. Bosch LE Jetronic fuel injection. Bore 95 mm, stroke 68.9 mm; capacity 2968 cc. Power 180 bhp (134 kW) at 5800 rpm; torque 182 lb ft (247 Nm) at 4800 rpm. Compression 9.4-to-1.

Transmission: Rear-wheel drive; five-speed manual gearbox is no-cost option. Four-speed automatic with lock-up torque converter standard. Top gear speed at 1000 rpm: 25.9 mph (41.7 km/h).

Suspension: Front, independent, MacPherson struts. Coil springs; telescopic dampers. Anti-roll bar. Rear, independent, semi-trailing arms and mini-block coil springs; telescopic dampers. Anti-roll bar.

Steering: Recirculating ball. Power assistance: standard.

Brakes: Ventilated discs front and rear, servo-assisted.

Tyres: 195/70-14.   **Fuel tank:** 15.4 Imp. gall (70 litres).

Dimensions: Length 190.5 in (4840 mm), width 67.7 in (1720 mm), height 55.7 in (1415 mm), wheelbase 105.7 in (2685 mm).

Unladen weight: 2998 lb (1360 kg).

Performance (Works): Maximum speed 130 mph (210 km/h); 0 to 60 mph (100 km/h) 9.0 sec. Fuel consumption at constant 75 mph (120 km/h): 18.9 mpg.

Features: Very luxuriously equipped. Air conditioning is standard on the CD. Electronic graphic intrumentation. Leather steering wheel cover. All Senators are now fitted with electronic anti-lock braking system.

VOLKSWAGEN (D)

Golf 1.6 GL

Identity: 'What car do *you* run?' people often ask me; well; here's the answer—the new Golf which was introduced Frankfurt 1983 (mainly a change of body), and on British market February 1985. Engine choice on British market starts with the 1043 cc Golf C; then 1272, 1595 petrol or diesel, and 1781 cc injection in GTI (page 183).

Engine: Front-mounted transverse four-cylinder with belt-driven single ohc and bucket tappets. Twin-choke carb. with automatic cold start enrichment and overrun fuel cut-off. Bore 81 mm, stroke 77.4 mm; capacity 1595 cc. Power 75 bhp (55 kW) at 5000 rpm; torque 90 lb ft (125 Nm) at 2500 rpm. Compression 9.0-to-1.

Transmission: Front-wheel drive; five-speed manual gearbox; fifth is high gear labelled E for economy; automatic optional. Top gear speed at 1000 rpm: 23.8 mph (38.3 km/h).

Suspension: Front, independent, MacPherson struts and coil springs; telescopic dampers. Anti-roll bar. Rear, independent, trailing arms and coil springs; telescopic dampers.

Steering: Rack and pinion. Power assistance: not available.

Brakes: Discs front, drums rear, servo-assisted.

Tyres: 175/70 SR 13.   **Fuel tank:** 12.1 Imp. gall (55 litres).

Dimensions: Length 156.9 in (3985 mm), width 65.6 in (1665 mm), height 55.7 in (1415 mm), wheelbase 97.4 in (2475 mm).

Unladen weight: 1962 lb (890 kg).

Performance *Autocar* test: Maximum speed 102 mph (164 km/h); 0 to 60 mph (100 km/h) 10.9 sec. Fuel consumption at constant 75 mph (120 km/h): 34.9 mpg; overall test, 29.9 mpg.

Features: Four-door hatchback body. Very efficient car with high gearing for effortless cruising with good economy. Neat interior finish.

VOLKSWAGEN (D)   Golf GTi

Identity: GTi version of the new Golf followed the modified range which was introduced at Frankfurt 1983. More space with the new larger body, but a little heavier than the previous version. Still one of the pace-setters in the hot-hatchback market.

Engine: Front-mounted transverse four-cylinder with belt-drive ohc. Alloy head. Bosch K-Jetronic fuel injection. Bore 81 mm, stroke 86.4 mm; capacity 1781 cc. Power 112 bhp (84 kW) at 5800 rpm; torque 109 lb ft (151 Nm) at 3500 rpm. Compression 10.0-to-1.

Transmission: Front-wheel drive; five-speed manual gearbox; no automatic option. Top gear speed at 1000 rpm: 20.2 mph (32.5 km/h).

Suspension: Front, independent, MacPherson struts, coil springs; telescopic dampers. Anti-roll bar. Rear, independent, trailing arms, coil springs; telescopic dampers.

Steering: Rack and pinion. Power assistance: not available.

Brakes: Ventilated discs front, drums rear, servo-assisted.

Tyres: 185/60 HR-14.   **Fuel tank:** 12.1 Imp. gall (55 litres).

Dimensions: Length 156.9 in (3985 mm), width 66.1 in (1680 mm), height 55.3 in (1405 mm), wheelbase 97.4 in (2475 mm).

Unladen weight: 2028 lb (920 kg).

Performance *Autocar* test: Maximum speed 114 mph (183 km/h); 0 to 60 mph (100 km/h) 8.6 sec. Fuel consumption at constant 75 mph (120 km/h): 25.9 mpg; overall test, 29.0 mpg.

Features: The extra weight means the new GTi is a little slower in acceleration, but it still has a smooth and willing engine in a car with delightful handling. Two-door hatchback body coming later in same body style in convertible form. On-board computer for fuel consumption and other functions, standard.

VOLKSWAGEN (D)   Jetta Formel E

Identity: Jetta is the booted version of the Golf, and it, too, has had a complete revision of bodywork like its hatchback sister. The boot is claimed to be the largest capacity of any production saloon car. Three petrol engines, and one diesel model are offered. New model (launched June 1984) much roomier inside.

Engine: Front-mounted transverse four-cylinder with belt-driven ohc. Two-stage carburettor. Bore 75 mm, stroke 72 mm; capacity 1275 cc. Power 55 bhp (41 kW) at 5400 rpm; torque 71 lb ft (96 Nm) at 3300 rpm. Compression 9.5-to-1.

Transmission: Front-wheel drive; four-speed manual gearbox, with fourth a high, economy ratio. Top gear speed at 1000 rpm: 19.07 mph (30.7 km/h).

Suspension: Front, independent, MacPherson struts and coil springs; telescopic dampers. Anti-roll bar. Rear, independent, MacPherson struts, torsion beam trailing arm axle with track adjustment bearings.

Steering: Rack and pinion. Power assistance: not available.

Brakes: Discs front, drums rear, servo-assisted.

Tyres: 175/70 SR-13.   **Fuel tank:** 12.1 Imp. gall (55 litres).

Dimensions: Length 170 in (4315 mm), width 66 in (1665 mm), height 56 in (1415 mm), wheelbase 97 in (2475 mm).

Unladen weight: 1973 lb (895 kg).

Performance (Works): Maximum speed 93 mph (150 km/h); 0 to 60 mph (100 km/h) 16.4 sec. Fuel consumption at constant 75 mph (120 km/h): 39.2 mpg.

Features: Main asset of the Jetta is its generous boot, with a claimed capacity of 23 cu ft. The Formel E version has a fuel consumption indicator, gear change up tell-tale and the special VW 'stop-start' system.

VOLKSWAGEN (D)   Passat 4 × 4

Identity: Although the four-wheel drive Passat was first shown Frankfurt 1983, it has yet to arrive on British market. Introduction now expected in 1985, when new system of four-wheel drive will appear in this roomy four-door estate car.

Engine: Front-mounted longitudinal five-cylinder with belt-driven single ohc. Bosch K-Jetronic fuel injection. Alloy head. Bore 81 mm, stroke 77.4 mm; capacity 1994 cc. Power 113 bhp (85 kW) at 5400 rpm; torque 119 lb ft (164 Nm) at 3200 rpm. Comp. 10.0-to-1.

Transmission: Four-wheel drive; five-speed manual gearbox; permanent drive to all wheels. No automatic transmission option. Top gear speed at 1000 rpm: 25.4 mph (40.9 km/h).

Suspension: Front, independent, MacPherson struts and coil springs; telescopic dampers. Anti-roll bar. Rear, independent, semi-trailing arms and coil springs; telescopic dampers. Anti-roll bar.

Steering: Rack and pinion. Power assistance: standard.

Brakes: Vented discs front, solid discs rear, servo-assisted.

Tyres: 195/60 R 14.   **Fuel tank:** 15.4 Imp. gall (70 litres).

Dimensions: Length 174.6 in (4435 mm), width 66.3 in (1685 mm), height 54.5 in (1385 mm), wheelbase 100.4 in (2550 mm).

Unladen weight: 2789 lb (1265 kg).

Performance (Works): Maximum speed 113 mph (182 km/h); 0 to 60 mph (100 km/h) 11.1 sec. Fuel consumption at constant 75 mph (120 km/h): 29.1 mpg.

Features: First launched as the Passat Tetra, this 4 × 4 model will now be known as the Passat Variant syncro. Good space and equipment; lockable front and rear diffs. Divided rear seat; aerodynamically designed roof rack is available.

VOLKSWAGEN (D)   Passat GL5

Identity: In March 1985, Volkswagen abandoned the name Santana in UK, and this top model of the range became the Passat saloon, with choice of 1.6-, 1.8- and 2.0-litre engines. Top model is the GL5 (details follow).

Engine: Front-mounted in-line five-cylinder with belt-driven ohc. Bosch K-Jetronic fuel injection. Bore 81 mm, stroke 77.4 mm; capacity 1994 cc. Power 115 bhp (86 kW) at 5400 rpm; torque 120 lb ft (163 Nm) at 3200 rpm. Compression 10.1-to-1.

Transmission: Front-wheel drive; five-speed manual gearbox; fifth is geared-up for economy (4 + E). Automatic is an option. Top gear speed at 1000 rpm: 25.4 mph (40.8 km/h).

Suspension: Front, independent, MacPherson struts and coil springs; telescopic dampers. Anti-roll bar. Rear, dead beam torsion crank axle on trailing arms, with coil springs; telescopic dampers.

Steering: Rack and pinion. Power assistance: standard.

Brakes: Discs front, drums rear, servo-assisted.

Tyres: 195/60 HR-14.   **Fuel tank:** 13.2 Imp. gall (60 litres).

Dimensions: Length 178.9 in (4545 mm), width 66.7 in (1695 mm), height 55.1 in (1400 mm), wheelbase 100.4 in (2550 mm).

Unladen weight: 2480 lb, (1125 kg).

Performance (Works): Maximum speed 114 mph (184 km/h); 0 to 60 mph (100 km/h) 10.5 sec. Fuel consumption at constant 75 mph (120 km/h): 38.2 mpg.

Features: Front spoiler and sports alloy wheels distinguish the GX5 model. This top model has central locking on all doors, boot and filler cap, and electrically operated windows all round. Comfortable, roomy car with generous specification.

VOLKSWAGEN (D)   Polo

Identity: Smallest model in the Volkswagen range. An economical and versatile small car with almost estate-car-like carrying capacity. Also available in Coupé form.

Engine: Front-mounted transverse four-cylinder with belt-driven ohc. Alloy head. Bore 74 mm, stroke 59 mm; capacity 1043 cc. Power 40 bhp (29.5 kW) at 5300 rpm; torque 54 lb ft (100 Nm) at 2700 rpm. Compression 9.5-to-1.

Transmission: Front-wheel drive; four-speed manual gearbox. Top gear speed at 1000 rpm: 16.4 mph (26.4 km/h).

Suspension: Front, independent, MacPherson struts and coil springs; telescopic dampers. Anti-roll bar. Rear, semi-independent, trailing arms and torsion beam; telescopic dampers.

Steering: Rack and pinion. Power assistance: not available.

Brakes: Discs front, drums rear, servo-assisted.

Tyres: 145 SR-13.   **Fuel tank:** 7.9 Imp. gall (36 litres).

Dimensions: Length 143.9 in (3655 mm), width 62.2 in (1580 mm), height 53.3 in (1355 mm), wheelbase 91.9 in (2335 mm).

Unladen weight: 1543 lb (700 kg).

Performance *Autocar* test: Maximum speed 85 mph (136 km/h); 0 to 60 mph (100 km/h) 17.9 sec. Fuel consumption at constant 75 mph (120 km/h): 34.0 mpg; overall test, 35.0 mpg.

Features: Unusual shape for a supermini, more an estate than a hatchback. Efficient little car, taut and with a responsive engine. Available with a Formel E version and as notchback saloon, the Polo Classic.

VOLKSWAGEN (D)   Scirocco Storm

Identity: Special conversion of the Scirocco GTi by coachbuilders Karmann of Osnabruck, Germany. At first, Storm was clearly identified from the standard Scirocco by its skirts and front/rear spoilers; but revised range launched Paris 1984 saw similar embellishments introduced for ordinary Scirocco GTi. Look for Storm badge on rear.

Engine: Front-mounted transverse four-cylinder with belt-driven ohc. Bosch K-Jetronic fuel injection. Alloy head. Bore 81 mm, stroke 86.4 mm; capacity 1781 cc. Power 112 bhp (82 kW) at 5900 rpm; torque 112.5 lb ft (153 Nm) at 3500 rpm. Compression 10.0-to-1.

Transmission: Front-wheel drive; five-speed manual gearbox; no automatic option. Top gear speed at 1000 rpm: 23.6 mph (38 km/h).

Suspension: Front, independent, MacPherson struts and coil springs; telescopic dampers. Anti-roll bar. Rear, independent, torsion beam and trailing arms, with coil springs; telescopic dampers. Anti-roll bar.

Steering: Rack and pinion. Power assistance: not available.

Brakes: Discs front, drums rear, servo-assisted.

Tyres: 185/60 HR 14.   **Fuel tank:** 8.8 Imp. gall (40 litres).

Dimensions: Length 160.8 in (4084 mm), width 64 in (1626 mm), height 50.4 in (1280 mm), wheelbase 94.4 in (2398 mm).

Unladen weight: 1973 lb (895 kg).

Performance *Autocar* test: Maximum speed 116 mph (187 km/h); 0 to 60 mph (100 km/h) 9.0 sec. Fuel consumption at constant 75 mph (120 km/h): 39.2 mpg; overall test, 25.5 mpg.

Features: Delightful car to drive, and very generously equipped with leather trim for seats, doors and side panels. Electric window lifts and— as for GTi—trip computer with column changeover switch is standard. Excellent handling, helped by larger tyres on alloy wheels.

VOLVO (S)

360 GLE Injection

Identity: Volvo extended the 3-series range in 1983 with introduction of the saloon versions, designated GLE. The hatchback versions continue. The saloons are available with either carburettor or fuel injected versions of the 2-litre engine. Completely new engine with low internal friction introduced September 1984.

Engine: Front-mounted longitudinal four-cylinder with chain-driven single ohc. Bosch LE Jetronic fuel injection. Bore 88.9 mm, stroke 80 mm; capacity 1986 cc. Power 115 bhp (85 kW) at 5700 rpm; torque 118 lb ft (160 Nm) at 4200 rpm. Compression 10.1-to-1.

Transmission: Rear-wheel drive; five-speed manual gearbox (in transaxle at rear of car). Top gear speed at 1000 rpm: 23.5 mph (37.8 km/h).

Suspension: Front, independent, MacPherson struts and coil springs; telescopic dampers. Anti-roll bar. Rear, De Dion layput with trailing arms, semi-elliptic leaf springs and telescopic dampers.

Steering: Rack and pinion.

Brakes: Discs front, drums rear, servo-assisted.

Tyres: 175/70 R 13.   **Fuel tank:** 12.5 Imp. gall (57 litres).

Dimensions: Length 173.8 in (4415 mm), width 65.4 in (1660 mm), height 54.8 in (1392 mm), wheelbase 94.5 in (2400 mm).

Unladen weight: 2414 lb (1095 kg).

Performance (Works): Maximum speed 112 mph (180 km/h); 0 to 60 mph (100 km/h) 12.0 sec. Fuel consumption at constant 75 mph (120 km/h): 36.7 mpg.

Features: High level of standard equipment including central locking and tinted glass. Injection model can be identified by the fog lamps in front spoiler.

VOLVO (S) 240 estate car

Identity: Big and very roomy estate car body in Volvo's 240 series now has the 240 name (previously 245), and was changed in 1983 by introduction of a five-speed gearbox with aluminium casing. It is fitted in examples with the carburettor engine; injection versions retain a four-speed gearbox plus electrically-controlled separate overdrive unit.

Engine: Front-mounted longitudinal four-cylinder with belt-driven ohc. Alloy head. Zenith carburettor. Bore 96 mm, stroke 80 mm; capacity 2316 cc. Power 110 bhp (82 kW) at 5000 rpm; torque 134 lb ft (185 Nm) at 2500 rpm. Compression 10.3-to-1.

Transmission: Rear-wheel drive; five-speed manual gearbox; four-speed automatic transmission with high top ratio, optional. Top gear speed at 1000 rpm: 24.6 mph (39.6 km/h).

Suspension: Front, independent, MacPherson struts; coil springs and telescopic dampers. Anti-roll bar. Rear, live axle on trailing arms with Panhard rod; coil springs and telescopic dampers. Anti-roll bar.

Steering: Rack and pinion. Power assistance: optional (standard on GLE).

Brakes: Discs front and rear, servo-assisted.

Tyres: 185 SR 14. **Fuel tank:** 13.2 Imp. gall (60 litres).

Dimensions: Length 188.6 in (4790 mm), width 67.3 in (1710 mm), height 57.6 in (1462 mm), wheelbase 103.9 in (2640 mm).

Unladen weight: 2921 lb (1325 kg).

Performance (Works): Maximum speed 106 mph (171 km/h); 0 to 60 mph (100 km/h) 12.5 sec. Fuel consumption at constant 75 mph (120 km/h): 29.7 mpg.

Features: Bulky but very competent load carrier, not too heavy to drive and with usual rear seat folding provision. Optional rearward facing seat.

VOLVO (S)   740 GL

Identity: Volvo's big but ungainly saloon first appeared in early 1982 with a V6 petrol injection engine or turbo diesel. For 1985 Volvo extended the range to include three models using the smaller 2.3-litre four-cylinder engine and a lower specification level.

Engine: Front-mounted in-line four-cylinder with belt-drive ohc. Alloy head. Bore 96 mm, stroke 80 mm; capacity 2316 cc. Power 114 bhp (84 kW) at 5200 rpm; torque 141 lb ft (192 Nm) at 2500 rpm. Compression 10.3-to-1.

Transmission: Rear-wheel drive; five-speed manual gearbox; four-speed automatic with overdrive option. Top gear speed at 1000 rpm: 24.6 mph (39.6 km/h).

Suspension: Front, independent, MacPherson struts, coil springs and telescopic dampers. Anti-roll bar. Rear, live axle located by pivoted subframe and trailing arms, coil springs and telescopic dampers. Anti-roll bar.

Steering: Rack and pinion. Power assistance: standard.

Brakes: Discs front and rear, servo-assisted.

Tyres: 185/70-14.   **Fuel tank:** 13.2 Imp. gall (60 litres).

Dimensions: Length 188.5 in (4788 mm), width 69.3 in (1760 mm), height 56.3 in (1430 mm), wheelbase 109.1 in (2771 mm).

Unladen weight: 2866 lb (1300 kg).

Performance (Works): Maximum speed 113 mph (182 km/h); 0 to 60 mph (100 km/h) 10.9 sec. Fuel consumption at constant 75 mph (120 km/h): 32.5 mpg.

Features: Very similar to its bigger engined brothers, the 740 retains a high level of standard specification including central locking and heated driver and passenger front seats.

YUGO (YU)

Identity: When this Yugoslavian make first arrived in Britain it offered only a licence-built version of the obsolete Fiat 128; but the 45, launched at Birmingham 1982, offers more appeal and individuality. Acceptably roomy three-door body and more modern design concept, to which the respected Porsche engineers contributed.

Engine: Front-mounted transverse four-cylinder with pushrod ohv. Alloy head. Weber carb. Only three main bearings. Bore 65 mm, stroke 68 mm; capacity 903 cc. Power 45 bhp (33.5 kW) at 5800 rpm; torque 46 lb ft (64 Nm) at 3300 rpm. Compression 9.0-to-1.

Transmission: Front-wheel drive; four-speed manual gearbox; final drive 4.08-to-1. Top gear speed at 1000 rpm: 15.8 mph (25.4 km/h).

Suspension: Front, independent, MacPherson struts; coil springs and telescopic dampers. Anti-roll bar. Rear, independent. swinging lower arms and upper transverse leaf spring, which provides anti-roll effect. Telescopic dampers.

Steering: Rack and pinion. Power assistance: not available.

Brakes: Discs front, drums rear, servo-assisted.

Tyres: 145 SR 13.   **Fuel tank:** 6.6 Imp. gall (30 litres).

Dimensions: Length 137.4 in (3490 mm), width 60.7 in (1542 mm), height 54.7 in (1389 mm), wheelbase 84.6 in (2149 mm).

Unladen weight: 1595 lb (725 kg).

Performance *Autocar* test: Maximum speed 84 mph (135 km/h); 0 to 60 mph (100 km/h) 20.9 sec. Fuel consumption at constant 75 mph (120 km/h): 35.8 mpg; overall test 38.0 mpg.

Features: Modest equipment and rather basic trim but GL gets alloy wheels with larger tyres, and has tweed cloth upholstery. Handling much better than might be expected with a swing axle design.